The Harcombe Year

This book, which charts a year on a somewhat eccentric Cotswold farm, is for our large family and also for our adopted family of the girls who ride or keep their horses here and who are so much part of the Harcombe scene. It is also for the people who come to help us out now we aren't as young and agile as we once were and for our neighbours who are also our friends. Not forgetting the animals who add such joy to our lives, but particularly for Malcolm without whom none of this would happen.

Acknowledgements

My thanks to Jeremy Brookes, Emily Brown, Christopher Fear, Lorna Gray, Ross Matthews, Ian Street and Simon Turner for their lovely photographs. Also to the Rev Canon Andrew Bowden for giving me access to the "Gloucestershire Wassail", to June Lewis-Jones for telling me about the origins of both cheese rolling and wassailing and to Eric Freeman for his description of wassailing 'from the horse's mouth'.

Chapters

Appendix

Poems and Plates

The Cast

Malcolm - *husband*
Johnny and Christine - *brother-in-law and sister-in-law*
Anne - *sister-in-law*

Children & step-children

Kate and Simon - *daughter and partner*
Em - *daughter*
Sally and Antony - *step-daughter and husband*
Maggie - *step-daughter*
Liz and Ian - *step-daughter and fiancé*
Ross and Jess - *step-son and partner*

Grandchildren

Daisy and Ruby - *Em's daughters*
Amelia - *Liz and Ian's daughter*
Ollie - *step-grandson*
Jimbo and Jess - *Maggie's son and girlfriend*

Visitors to the yard

Eliza, Young Emily, Maddi, Chloe, Molly and Jack - *the Harcombe*

Lorna, Peta, Susan and her parents Derek and Lesley, Natasha and her mum Hazel - *the Livery girls*

Amelia - *riding instructor*

Mike and Elise - *our trusted vets*

David and Alex - *our dependable farriers*

Friends, neighbours and extended family

Catherine and Gordon, Stephen, Phil and Gay, Penny and Andrew, Sue and Andrew - *the neighbours*

Saus, Brian and Cathy, Jeremy, Richard and Barry - *the helpers*

Janine, Littie (Em's godmother), Louise, Charlotte, Granny Jane, Val, Sharon and Ben, Heather and Mike, Ada and Istvan, David and Cleota, Heila and Lucy, Jim and Gena, Michael and Davnet - *the friends*

Aubrey, Auntie Nora, Cousin Jessie, Claire, Martin and Hilary - *the family*

Animals

Charlie, Freddie, Splash, Jessie, Pandora, William, Rosie and Bilbo - *the horses and ponies*

Gypsy and MooMoo - *the dogs*

Percy, Freya, Pumpkin and Baggie - *the cats*

Nancy, Pamela, Jessica and Deborah - *the hens*

Cracker, Bubs and Titch - *the goats*

A cold coming we had of it,
Just the worst time of the year
For a journey, and such a long journey:
The ways deep and the weather sharp,
The very dead of winter.

T S Eliot - *The Journey of the Magi*

Harcombe Wood

January

Another New Year, full of hope and promise. Only this year initially it seemed neither hopeful nor promising. Nor even new. The same old soggy weather which had made last year the wettest since records began hung on and on, turning the rural Cotswold landscape to dreary shades of brown and grey with skies so low and dark that they seemed to be resting on the top of the beech trees in Harcombe Wood.

Then suddenly, inexplicably, the odd day of bright sunshine and clear blue skies lights the skeleton trees on the horizon and makes me remember why I love the winter. And it's the season of Epiphany, the time when the wise men followed the star to find the infant Jesus. We tend to forget when singing that lovely hymn, 'As with gladness, men of old, Did the guiding star behold...' that it isn't really a Christmas carol but celebrates Epiphany – a new beginning and, whatever the weather, a time of hope.

It's also a time of wonderful winter surprises. When walking Gypsy along the side of Harcombe Wood, a fox the colour of mahogany poked out his nose, saw us and decided on another route, but not before he had given me the thrill I always have when I glimpse one of these wild and elegant creatures. Another day I saw two fallow deer silhouetted on the skyline at the top of Harcombe Valley and hastily changed direction before Gypsy spotted them too. Compared to all the other dogs we have had she is very good at not chasing moving creatures but deer are too much of a temptation.

Then at last, after two days of hard frost which had put the water taps in the stable yard out of action, came the snow. Not softly, not gently, but in storm mode, with wind blowing it into weirdly shaped drifts and into every nook and cranny – even between the cracks in the ponies' stable, a stone building which started life as a cowshed. Looking out on that first morning, it didn't seem too bad. I could even see the black of the road surface in some places. Even so, the thought of mucking out stables, taking feed and hay to the ponies who live out all the year round and filling frozen water buckets with watering cans carried from the house, didn't fill me with great enthusiasm.

A call from Jack, just as I was pulling on extra layers, reminded me that most clouds really do have silver linings. "School's closed, Di, could you do with some help?" "That's the best news I've had today," I told him. Jack is our neighbours' grandson and often – bravely – joins the gang of girls who come to ride and help with the ponies. Telling Malcolm that on no account

Testing the slippery-ness of the road with Gypsy

must he cross the road until I'd tested its slippery-ness (after all, he'd been boasting that he would be 81 the following day and there are a few regulations relating to old age) I slithered across the road and met Jack in the stable yard. When we'd mixed the feeds we set off to Splash and Jessie, walking through what was by now several inches of snow. Jessie stood by the gate in all her skewbald beauty, having chosen last night somehow to wriggle out of her rug. She was quite unrepentant and I was tempted to leave her like that but knew that by the evening my conscience would be pricking me. So when Jack and I had trudged back to the farm, I collected another rug (no chance of finding the original in all this snow) and slithered back with it – there was no sign of our outgoing footprints. And back again to the farm, to find Jack, bless him, hard at work.

Everything seems to take twice as long in the snow and we spent most of the day carting water and clearing snow, plus dealing with one of the livery ponies since her owner Natasha, whose mum Hazel drives her over each day, could not get out of Cirencester. Oh, hell, I thought, I don't fancy days and days of this.

But, of course, it wasn't like that at all. Next day more of the gang joined Jack on the yard, we fixed up a system which made carrying water much easier and we celebrated Malcolm's birthday safe and warm at home. David the postman had struggled through the snow bringing cards and parcels and Liz, Ian and Amelia managed to get here with a birthday cake. On Sunday Hazel appeared and insisted on helping me with the horses in return for my help on the previous days. An air of jollity and goodwill, which I always associate with rural snowfall, prevailed.

The forecasters seemed to think that we had seen the last of the snow but this turned out not to be the case. A few days later there was an even heavier fall though somehow it was less disruptive. But my next worry was the fact that Em, Daisy and Ruby were due to come for the weekend to celebrate Em's birthday and the snow seemed to be heading north towards them. In the event she decided to come, rather than be snowed in at home and I spent three anxious hours until they turned up, all triumph and smiles, on the doorstep. It really was 'the worst time of the year for a journey, and such a long journey' but it was as well that Em had grasped the nettle – a friend from home sent her a photograph just after she arrived to show several inches of snow in their street – and we had one of the most fun weekends ever.

Nor could I blame Em for her determination since it was one of the things that we taught both she and Kate as children. We always lived in a rural spot and yet we never sat back and stayed indoors when the snow fell, which it did much more frequently a quarter of a century ago. My children had some of the best school attendance records, although we lived almost the furthest away, and getting them even to the school bus (which nearly always ran in those days) involved some hazardous journeys over the years. But it was what we did before everyone seemed to get soft and fearful and schools closed if a lone snowflake came drifting down. And we still remember the times when we dug and pushed Brian's car up and out of our drive as he made his determined way to work. Every day.

Did it do us any harm? Absolutely not. And the best thing about it is that Daisy and Ruby are being brought up not to be fearful either. They thought their trip from the north, being chased by snowstorms, the very greatest adventure but Em admitted later that she had moments of panic as the snow occasionally caught up with them. I know about those.

Luckily we had held the Gloucestershire Farmers' Friends' first meeting of the year before the snow closed in and temporarily put an end to anyone (except Em) venturing very far afield. The Farmers' Friends was founded by Malcolm nearly a quarter of a century ago when it became very obvious that farming had changed drastically, mainly due to the use of sophisticated agricultural equipment. This had meant that groups of men were no longer employed on farms and the job of the farmer became a very lonely one. Moreover, the amalgamation of small farms which had happened over the years, meant that the farmer now had few neighbours to help him out in a crisis or simply give a helping hand at busy times of the year, such as harvest.

Our slogan is 'Need a Neighbour? We are here.' And that just about sums it up. The difference between the Farmers' Friends and the Samaritans is that we don't try to sort out cases over the telephone, we actually go to the farm and if we can't solve it ourselves we get the appropriate professional help.

From small beginnings in Gloucestershire, the Farmers' Friends has been extraordinarily successful and branches now operate all over the country. Over the years Malcolm and his wonderful successor, Chris, have been called upon to give advice to those about to set up similar groups. The great strength of the Gloucestershire group is that we don't deal with money, therefore we have no overheads. If money is needed it can always be found, but those groups which have relied on grants and charged for services have tended to be less successful. Nevertheless, the organisation is flourishing countrywide and it all began here at Harcombe, thanks to Malcolm's vision.

But we like to enjoy ourselves and we are also good friends with one another so, in between helping the farming community we meet four times a year at the home of different members to discuss cases and future plans and then to have a jolly good feast. At one time about eight of us would sit down together, now it can be up to fifteen including several young people who will carry on helping farmers when the rest of us are probably needing help ourselves...

Malcolm and Em are not the only ones with January birthdays, for horses have an official birthday of January 1 and this year my beautiful Charlie has reached the grand old age of 32. He doesn't look it and he doesn't want to be reminded of it but the date 1981 is clearly printed on his passport, which all horses must now possess as an ongoing record of their lives. During the time I have owned ponies (which was not until I was grown up, in spite of continually nagging my poor parents) I have made a few mistakes but the majority have been what we wanted them to be – eventually.

Charlie, however, is the equine love of my life. We have been together since he was nine years old, when I insisted on buying him in spite of advice from a friend that he was too small. Too small! If he had been any bigger I wouldn't have been able to

Charlie is first to greet all visitors to the yard

control him at all. As it was, when I first had him, he was ready to run off if I so much as shifted in the saddle or gently blew my nose. I am not a good rider, I learned to ride on the endless beach at Blackpool, where I grew up. Not being able to stop the ponies which my cousin Hilary and I rode whenever we got the chance was a frequent hazard, so Charlie's early capers never fazed me and gradually, through mutual trust, they ceased altogether and when we galloped it was because we both wanted to. His nervousness also diminished as he trusted me more and more and, for me, he was the perfect pony, though this opinion wasn't shared by all those who rode him. In the very early days when either Kate or Em had taken him out for a ride, I overheard one say to the other, "Heavens, Mum must have improved to be able to deal with him." And it was true. He taught me at least as much as I taught him.

And he is one of the most handsome ponies I have ever owned. Partly Arabian and partly native Connemara, he holds his head and his tail high and steps out, even now, with an energy which belies his years. Once iron grey and dappled, he is now white as the snow which we have seen rather too much of recently but has lost none of his beauty. His stable is nearest to the yard gate, and one of the first things which visitors see when arriving at Harcombe is his handsome head, ears pricked, looking over the stable door. Anne, Malcolm's sister, who was born at Harcombe, says the farm won't be the same when he's no longer around. But please may that time not be yet.

Now the snow has largely gone, though the patches that remain remind me of the old saying that while there is still snow lying on the Cotswolds there is more to come.

But guess what. It's swilling with rain again.

When icicles hang by wall
And Dick the shepherd blows his nail,
And Tom brings logs into the hall,
And milk comes frozen home in pail;
When blood is nipped, and ways be foul,
Then nightly sings the staring owl
Tu-whoo!
Tu-whit! Tu-whoo! A merry note!
While greasy Joan doth keel the pot.

William Shakespeare ~ *Love's Labours Lost*

Icicles in the yard

February

I've never liked February. Somehow I always expect it to be the herald of spring but it seldom is – except for that rare, almost warm, sunny day which fools you into thinking that spring might just be on the way, only to have your hopes dashed by icy blasts the next. It's the time when, even if you've escaped colds and coughs all winter, you get them then – just when you're beginning to feel lucky. When I was at boarding school in the 1950s our teenage spots were at their worst in February and the dormitories echoed nightly with the sound of hollow coughing.

This February was the most unpleasant I can ever remember, with iron hard frosts, bitterly cold winds or driving rain. Like January before it, it hardly ever seemed to get properly light. Because Harcombe is so high, we get the worst of the weather but we also get dramatic wild skies with scudding clouds and a firmament of stars on frosty nights. Not this year, though, just low cloud, all the time.

On the very odd night, though, when there was a hard frost and a clear sky, we could hear the owls hooting in Harcombe Valley. Walking down there in the pale, cold moonlight, the steep valley sides white and glistening, we listened as one owl hooted and another answered, followed by another and another, until the still, cold air was alive with a cacophony of sound. Tu-whit! Tu-whoo! Indeed. It's a mystical experience and one not to be missed because it doesn't happen very often.

I developed a cough, followed by a cold. Then Malcolm got it. I felt better for a few days and then started coughing and sniffing again. So did he. We were both beginning to recover from this sorry state of affairs when our Stanley stove, which provides central heating and hot water, went out and refused to come back to life. The heating engineers said it would take

Fog clings to the valley after a rare frosty night

them a week to get a new part – that sounded bad enough but in fact it took over two weeks to mend. I never remember feeling so cold in my life – electric heaters and even our wood burning stove were no substitute for Stanley, who stood cold and sad in his corner of the kitchen. We also had a lot of visitors at that time and we seemed to spend ages running from room to room carrying electric radiators which only just managed to take the chill off the air. It was a great day when Stanley leapt back to life and I shall never again complain that Malcolm has the heating on too high. Not till the weather warms up anyway.

Even this cloud had a silver lining, however. Em, on a visit during Stanley's demise was so incensed to discover that the job hadn't been completed more quickly that she went on the internet and found a company which supplied Stanley parts. When I telephoned them I was assured that they could have supplied the part – which had taken two weeks to procure – within twenty four hours... I resolved to find a new heating engineer and after some research I discovered Barry who promised to come and look at Stanley who, we had been assured by those who were supposed to know, was almost at the end of his natural life. Dear Barry gave Stanley a thorough examination and reckoned that he could keep him ticking along, probably for another ten years. Since then he has breathed new life into the very sulky and temperamental central heating boiler in the cottage next door and has promised to service the boilers in three other houses which we rent out. This experience has convinced me to steer away from large companies in future and find someone who works for him or herself to do the job.

But we mostly do this anyway through a group of people who are almost literally on our doorstep. Saus (real name Anthony) makes very smart kitchens in the old granary opposite the house. He revamped our kitchen twenty years ago and it's still admired today. He also built us a beautiful balcony which leads out of our sitting room, where we sit and enjoy a drink or two on hot summer days (what are those?). He comes to help out when something more minor needs attention and from time to time he takes Malcolm to the pub with several of our other helpers.

One of these is Brian who lives in nearby Winstone and who can turn his hand to virtually anything from clearing out gutters to mending broken lavatories – and he's also your man when you've locked yourself out of your house or car. So is Saus, come to that, they'd both make very efficient burglars. Brian and his wife, Cathy, also come to mow the lawns, help to chop wood, both where it has fallen and when it's piled up in the covered yard. Whenever something goes wrong, and Malcolm looks as if he might tackle it himself, I hear myself saying, "Why don't you ring Brian?" He's utterly reliable, always turns up and solves the problem. As we grow older, we simply couldn't manage without him.

Across the road, in a converted Dutch barn live Lorna and Jeremy who are also people of very many parts. Lorna, who keeps her two ponies, Rosie and Bilbo, at livery on the farm, helps me to sort out my computer, draws lifelike portraits of our animals and writes books in her free time. Jeremy is a skilled woodworker but also rebuilds bits of the stables when horses kick them down and can turn his hand to most other things. They also keep goats, not for milk or for breeding, but simply because they like goats. Goats have not been my favourite animal since I looked after two for friends when they were away. They were horrible goats, always regarding me with a disdainful look as they worked out how they would outwit me – and they nearly always succeeded.

But Lorna and Jeremy's goats are real characters – especially when they are herding them from several fields away to the stable yard where they spend part of their time among the horses – and I find that I really like them and have conversations with them when no one is looking. They used to occupy one of the stables but recently Jeremy has built them a goat house which adjoins Bilbo's stable. Bilbo loves sharing with the goats but, if he gets too exuberant, they now have a little doorway into an adjoining enclosure, where he can see them but not follow them. In short, Lorna and Jeremy are as eccentric as we are.

Just up the road, Richard has a workshop on his parents' farm. Richard can weld together a tractor part, service a car, diagnose any mechanical problem and sort out a broken down horsebox or trailer. He has rescued us from many a car crisis. One of his more bizarre rescues happened on a day when Malcolm was walking up the road and met a woman coming towards him, leading two donkeys – we see some unusual sights at Harcombe but not often donkeys. It transpired that she and her husband were travelling to Liverpool with the donkeys and the brakes

Titch may be the smallest of the Harcombe goats but he has the longest beard

on their trailer had burned out. They were parked in the lay-by at the top of our lane and someone – goodness knows who – had suggested that she took the donkeys, who were getting somewhat stressed, down to Harcombe where they were sure that the Whitakers would have somewhere to put them. "We can do better than that," said Malcolm when we had settled the donkeys in William's little paddock, and took the woman to see Richard who soon had the brakes sorted out and they were on their way to Liverpool in just over an hour. When she wrote to thank me the donkey owner said how she had despaired when the trailer had broken down in what seemed like the middle of nowhere but in no time at all the problem was fixed. Syde may be the second smallest village in England, but it's certainly got a lot of talent.

Another bright spot in an otherwise gloomy February was that Pandora came to join the Harcombe ponies and she has proved to be a real joy. She belongs to Young Emily who is very generous about her being ridden by the rest of the gang. Pandora is an old fashioned cob with feathered fetlocks and a temperament to die for. She has settled well already, sharing a field with Splash and Jessie, who boss her about, but she keeps her distance and her own council. She is a real Harcombe pony. Not flashy. Good around children. Just nice.

The first Saturday of the month was also this year's first meeting of the Harcombe Society which was started by Malcolm 45 years ago. It has its roots in the Cirencester Literary Society which originally met in a dreary public building in the town until Malcolm suggested that the members might be more comfortable in the sitting room at Harcombe. They and their successors have been coming ever since on the first Saturday of each winter month (except January which is too near Christmas) to enjoy an evening of erudition and conviviality. Our speakers do not now confine themselves to literature but expound as well on a variety of subjects in the realms of science, art, music, nature and anything else in which members are interested. Previous members who have addressed the Harcombe Society include film maker Michael Powell (of the Hollywood partnership of Powell and Pressburger) and the nation's favourite poet Jenny Joseph who is now old enough to wear purple and spit in the street.

February

So in February our neighbour Mick Ponting, a retired vet, gave an amazing illustrated talk about his journey on horseback with a party of students across the top of Outer Mongolia. Among his adventures was his success in saving a horse which had been bitten by a wolf and the wounds had gone sceptic. He wanted to put the horse down but the Buddhist tribesmen would not allow him to do so and to his great surprise it survived. Thereafter, wherever he went during the trip he was known as "the man who saved the wolf-bitten horse" – the story even reached the ears of the British ambassador. And Outer Mongolia looked so cold and unforgiving that we began to feel the Cotswolds in February might not be so bad after all.

Another February delight was the arrival of Em, Daisy and Ruby to spend Daisy's birthday with us. That day was, miraculously, almost spring-like with sunshine and blue sky and my greatest treat was to witness Em and Daisy going off riding together for the first time. Em rode Charlie, while Daisy has now really got the hang of naughty little William who is the light of her life. As Ruby and I walked behind them the years fell away and it could have been me going out riding with Em and her sister Kate – in the same swathe of Cotswold countryside more than three decades ago. Ruby announced that her legs were tired and the next thing I knew was that she had climbed a gate and was sitting on Charlie in front of Em, grinning delightedly. It was a magic moment.

Nature, too, though it can be so depressing (especially in February) always provides sights which lift the heart. Like the

History in the making (from left): Di on Rocket, Kate on Bowler and Em on Copper

day I was driving home up the steep and winding road to Syde village and, as I turned a corner, I was confronted by a carpet of snowdrops covering the bank. Had the cold weather encouraged our most popular winter wild flower to grow bigger or to spread itself more thickly on the ground or was it just in contrast to the iron greyness around it? Who knows and who cares? It was a truly beautiful sight.

Times as cold as these make us very conscious of the plight of wild animals when there is nothing around to eat. To this end, any leftover food – meaty scraps, anything that is well past its sell-by date or has spent too long in the deep freeze is put out for the foxes to eat and has completely disappeared by the next morning. The fox feeding spot is pretty close to where we keep our four hens and our thinking is that if the foxes find food so easily it's hardly worth the trouble of catching a noisy feathered creature and running the risk of being caught in the act. It's worked so far. Fingers crossed.

Because we have three cats, it's not a good idea to have a formal bird table, so we have one of those mesh tubes which you fill with peanuts and hang from a tree. Every day Malcolm fills it up and every day we are entertained by the activities of the feathered and sometimes furry creatures who visit it. When we spot the tube swinging wildly backwards and forwards we know that the resident squirrel is in action. He has a lot of fun but doesn't get much to eat unless he manages to dislodge the tube from the tree altogether, which isn't often. Pheasants are not usually noted for their brainpower but the ones who visit our garden are certainly not stupid. First they eat the peanuts which Malcolm has spilled on the ground when he fills the tube and then they sit and wait for the robins, bluetits and all the other little birds to drop some of the nuts which they greedily pull from the tube. There are some very fat pheasants in the garden at Harcombe.

But the greatest excitement comes when we look out of the window and see the spotted woodpecker swinging on the feeder, picking out the nuts. I can never get used to the fact that this really is a resident British bird – its red, black and white plumage makes it look far more exotic than any of our other feathered friends and although it's such a regular visitor, it's always a tremendous thrill to see it. Except for the bullying magpies, it is obviously cock of the roost among the garden birds who keep their distance until it has eaten its fill.

"When winter comes, can spring be far behind?" I'm an eternal optimist and my glass is almost always half full. As we get towards March and Easter, I'm full of hope for better things to come. But this year I'm not holding my breath.

Glossy sweet aconite has shown her gold
And strong, straight crocus spears, where late we knelt
To lodge their bulbs, are waiting to unfold.
The ragged rooks like tea-leaves in the sky
Straggle towards the earth with awkward grace;
A robin in a silver birch nearby
Thrusts up his carol through the naked lace.

Joyce Grenfell ~ *March Day, 1941*

The lane towards the farm

March

This year March came in like the proverbial lamb and left like one too. In between, however, the weather was more like a raging pride of lions than just a single one.

Spring seemed at first to have come early and the first weekend of the month was bright, fresh and sharp as only March can be. Our old friends Heather and Mike came on a flying visit which happily coincided with one from Kate and Simon, and Em, Daisy and Ruby. Harcombe was looking its springtime best and we had a great day of laughter and reminiscence.

Heather and I go back a very long way. We became close friends when we were students and it was through our friendship that she met Mike, her future husband. Heather's parents didn't approve of Mike, partly because he had dropped out of university but also because he didn't come from their home town of Bolton... Let's say that they would have found any reason to criticise him since they hadn't chosen him as a suitable husband for their daughter. Heather ran away from home and married Mike, wearing my wedding dress and being given away by Brian, my first husband. Not approving of Mike was probably the biggest mistake Heather's parents ever made. He returned to university, took a master's degree, followed by a PHD in ultrasonics – a very new science in the 1960s. He has spent a lifetime inventing ultrasonic devices, mainly for the medical industry at home and overseas, and for many years they have had their own factory in the grounds of their Devon farmhouse. They employ over 50 people, including two of their sons, and have recently won the Queen's Award for Industry among many other accolades. It's been very much a joint enterprise with Heather keeping the family afloat by running farmhouse holidays in the years that Mike was getting the business off the ground. It's a huge success story, very much deserved, and I'm just so glad that it has happened to such dear friends. Sadly, Heather never saw her father again and visited her mother just before she died. Whose was the greater loss?

In the evening retired orthopaedic surgeon Guy Rooker – who, coincidentally was instrumental in his department buying one of Mike's ultrasonic devices some years ago – talked to a packed Harcombe Society on The Anatomy of Leonardo da Vinci, probably one of the greatest geniuses the world had ever known. Kate had come specially to hear Guy – they go back a long way to the time when she was nanny to the Rooker children during her gap year and have remained friends ever since.

The glorious weather did not prove to be a portent of what

Harcombe farmhouse: home to the Harcombe Society

was to come. Far from it. From then on we endured wind, rain, hail and more snow; the cold seemed never ending. There was still snow remaining in hollows by the side of the road at Birdlip (always mentioned in reports during times of extreme weather) almost to the end of the month. So I was particularly pleased to drive up there one day and find it gone at last.

But the wintry weather had taken its toll. There had been crops pushing their way up through the soil in January, covering the fields in a film of green. Now there was only an expanse of brown mud and a lot of disappointed looking pigeons who love to descend on the new shoots at this time of year. The rooks had a hard time building their nests in the top of trees being buffeted by gale force winds and our hens simply fluffed out their feathers and looked at me as if I was mad when I mentioned that an occasional egg might be nice. Much, much worse was the fact that many lambs were lost through the snow, wet and bitter cold, including some belonging to Stephen, our neighbouring farmer, the son of our good friends, Gordon and Catherine.

Almost every Sunday Sally, Malcolm's eldest daughter, comes up from Cheltenham to see us. Sally is quite unlike her siblings who have inherited Malcolm's noisy, extravert personality. She is quiet, like her mother Judy, who was such a good friend of mine. Most Sundays Sally and I, while catching up on the week's news, take Gypsy for a walk, usually in Harcombe Wood, and this month we have been on the lookout for any signs of life there. Only towards the end did we spot the odd, very small, spike of a new bluebell or wild garlic leaf poking out of the soil and looking for the hint of a bud on any of the trees proved to be endlessly disappointing. But then, joy of joys, we saw a tiny primrose on the woodland track. Maybe there really will be a spring this year.

In Syde – though probably not in many other parishes – one of the high spots of March is the annual Parish Meeting which takes place in our sitting room at Harcombe. For many years Syde did not hold a Parish Meeting (the village is too small to merit anything as grand as a Parish Council) and everyone was, I understand, quite happy with that arrangement. Then, as a result of local government reorganisation, the people of Syde were told that if they didn't revive their Parish Meeting, the village would be amalgamated with neighbouring Brimpsfield and Caudle Green. Syde has a long tradition of independence and this proposal was not to be tolerated. The Parish Meeting was reinstated with Malcolm as its chairman and Harcombe as its meeting place and it has been going on here ever since.

What makes the Syde meeting different, probably from any other such gathering in the land, is that everyone brings a bottle of their preferred tipple, we get the business over quickly and then drink the contents of the bottles. This format ensures that we get an over 90 per cent attendance level and everyone leaves feeling good. We do have some fierce arguments but nothing that can't be solved over a glass of wine. As well as nearly all the people in the village being there, our district and county councillors seldom miss it. I recently read an email from the outgoing county councillor to his successor, advising him that our meeting was one not to miss. I think he described it as 'quirky' and he's right.

Towards the end of the month American visitors came to Harcombe – as they often do. Malcolm has made many friends from the US over the years but his oldest friend is David Tatham, now emeritus professor of fine arts at the University of Syracuse in New York State. David has visited England almost every year since the 1960s, originally to show the art treasures of Europe to his students, latterly because he and his wife, Cleota, love being in England. While making London their base, they come to stay with us, often bringing members of their family with them. This month they were due to visit with Cle's daughter, Heila, and granddaughter, Lucy, who we had never met before. In the end David and Cle couldn't come so Heila and Lucy arrived on their own and we had a lot of fun with them. Lucy was very keen to ride and, as the school holidays had just started, she was able to make friends with Young Emily, Maddi, Chloe and Molly who come to ride every Saturday and much more often when school's out.

Lucy had learned to ride but in Western style and was much teased by the others as they took her down to the ménage at Syde Manor, which the Neubauers who own it are kind enough to let us use, and taught her the mysteries of the rising trot. They made her laugh so much that she was in danger of sliding off Jessie's broad back, but she just managed to stay put. She is a lovely girl who fitted in very well at Harcombe and loved Gypsy and the cats as well as the ponies. She cried when it was time to go and we missed her a lot. Some time later a parcel arrived at the farm and in it was a box of cookies (biscuits to us) each one iced to look like the various ponies. They were very popular and didn't last long but I still have the one of Gypsy which Lucy made for me.

Easter fell at the end of March this year and Holy Week was the coldest and wettest of a particularly horrid month. Our new parson, Val, had organised a series of pilgrimage walks from parish to parish in her enormous benefice and I really had intended to join at least one of them. But it was so cold and wet and I spent so much time getting muddy, miserable ponies in from fields, turning them out again and walking an ever exuberant Gypsy through dripping, windy woods that I felt I had had enough exercise for one week. The pilgrimages, though, were a great success and ended in a Passover supper in the tythe barn at Syde Manor which we did attend and learned a lot about that particularly Jewish custom. And as usual I helped to make the traditional Easter Garden to put in the church on Easter Sunday, but even this bore the signs of what had been before. We were short of spring flowers and leafy branches and this year's garden looked more Good Friday than Easter Sunday – a poignant reminder of the last few weeks with only a hint of the promise of spring.

The last time Good Friday fell in March there were also hail storms. I remember it so well because Malcolm and I found two tiny lambs sheltering against the body of their dead mother. They would have been lucky to survive the night in such conditions and they made no protest when Malcolm caught them and bundled them into the back of the car. Clearly they had lived off their meagre body fat for a couple of days for the ewe had been dead for at least that long. We took them home, bedded them down in straw in one of the stables and set off for the feed merchants to buy milk substitutes and rubber teats. We also bought a tube to get milk into their stomachs in case they wouldn't suck.

We needn't have worried. Those lambs grabbed the teats and drank as if their life depended on it – which of course it did. Their little bodies expanded before our eyes and in no time they were snuggled down together in the warm straw. As a townie, born and bred, I was enthralled. Baby lambs for Easter and the grandchildren arriving tomorrow! Daisy and Ruby were ecstatic, especially as the lambs were so tiny that they were able to give them the bottles themselves. No other entertainment was needed and those lambs must have almost doubled their body weight with the constant meals being delivered to them. We racked our brains for names and finally came up with Wallace and Gromit which came more and more to suit the adventurous pair.

We knew – though we didn't tell Daisy and Ruby – that we couldn't keep them for ever. If they had been ewes, who would produce more lambs, it would have been different but they were a couple of little rams who became more and more boisterous as they grew older, nearly knocking me over when I arrived with the ever fuller bottles. We decided that it would be a good idea if they did a bit of work and trimmed the back lawn and we had some hilarious moments herding them across the road to the garden. They were not good lawn mowers, far preferring the young plants in my tubs and pots and eventually we decided that they had to go. Malcolm's cousin Aubrey, who has a flock of pedigree, prize winning Texel sheep, agreed to take them but what happened to them in the end I could never quite bring myself to ask.

Back to the present and Easter Sunday, the high spot in the Christian calendar. I cannot pretend to be as devout a Christian as I would like. I have had no Damascus Road experience. But that Jesus Christ was crucified on Good Friday and rose again on Easter Sunday in order to show us how to be His followers is at the centre of my belief and Easter, freed from the commercialism of Christmas, is a very special time. To spend an hour of that time in the tiny medieval church in Syde, the village where I have lived for so many happy years, singing the Easter hymns and taking part in the traditional communion service from the Book of Common Prayer is something that very little could make me miss. "Jesus Christ is risen today! Alleluia!"

Often in this service we are surrounded by animals and children, telling the Easter story. This year it was just a few of us since the actors, human and animal, had rather worn themselves out taking part in the wonderful Good Friday pageant in Syde and nearby Caudle Green, organised each year by retired rector Canon Andrew Bowden and his wife Sue. But those of us who were there on Easter Sunday felt, as always, the warmth and friendship which in recent years has become so much a part of this tiny Cotswold parish.

This Easter Sunday was also a big family occasion when Johnny and Chris's first grandchild, Julia, was baptised and this was followed by a party for the two families at their picture book cottage on the boundary of Syde and Caudle Green. Johnny and Chris's son Will is married to Hannah whose father is Palestinian, and to celebrate both a baptism and Easter with a group of people who originally came from the Holy Land was very special.

And the sun shone all day. Christ was risen indeed.

Loveliest of trees, the cherry now
Is hung with blooms along the bough,
And stands along the woodland ride
Wearing white for Eastertide.

A E Housman ~ *The Shropshire Lad*

cherry in Syde churchyard

April

The cold and often wet weather which has continued into April, combined with the early Easter, meant that the cherry tree in our garden was in no way wearing white for Eastertide – but those lines of Housman are so evocative that I just had to use them. And as the month progressed and the weather got a bit warmer, our tree blossomed in all its glory. It stands in the middle of the lawn and although it is now, like us, getting a bit elderly and doesn't bloom like it once did, it still makes a beautiful picture. Best of all, its message is that spring is here at last.

But not at the beginning of the month. However, slowly, slowly the evenings are getting lighter so I'm determined to be optimistic and look at all the good things because I'm well aware that the awful weather has been the dominating factor in my ramblings so far.

With this in mind Gypsy and I set off each day in positive

mood, heading for Harcombe Wood, looking for at least the promise of spring. And we found it. First in the celandines, their shiny yellow flowers defying the cold, then in the clumps of pale primroses blooming bravely, high up on the steep side of the wood at the entrance to our enormous badgers' sett.

Looking for the trees bursting into bud proved less successful – not even a hint of green on the enormous beeches, usually the first to show. No hope, then, for the ash which is always a late starter, no sticky buds on the chestnuts either. And in the hedgerows the blackthorn, which blossoms before its leaves appear, remained black and thorny.

I thought of the contrast of a day more than thirty years ago when Em and I were riding through nearby Miserden Park together. Spring had come early that year and the beech leaves were appearing almost as we watched. "Mummy, Mummy, it's just like green lace," cried ten year-old Em, making me realise, not for the first time, how fortunate we were that we didn't have a television and that our children could use their imagination to the full. As it turned out, it wasn't all blossom and green lace because that year we had a heavy fall of snow at the end of April and many branches broke through the weight of the snow on the leaves. Malcolm remembers the same garden cherry tree in full bloom and covered with snow –luckily it suffered no damage and provided, for a brief moment, a sight to live long in the memory. Housman would have approved.

Riding in Miserden Park, which we are so lucky to have so close, featured large during April, despite the weather, since

Daisy has now really got the bug and rode at least once on every day of the holiday they spent with us. She managed to ride, as well as her beloved William, all the other ponies except Splash, and including Charlie whom she rode very confidently with me walking or running beside her. Always something of a wild man, Charlie seems to have settled down in old age while still losing none of his sparkle. It was a good moment when Em and Daisy went off for their first 'proper' ride together, returning pink faced and smiling well over an hour later. How I wish I could have them for longer and that they could enjoy the unfettered, outdoor life that Em and Kate enjoyed when they were only a little older. I would find out the vague direction in which they intended to ride and off they would go (no mobile phones in those days), returning when they were hungry, relating their adventures, usually about the jumps they had tackled – tales which lost nothing in the telling.

On the final day of their holiday Daisy had the misfortune to have her toe trodden on by Jessie, by far the fattest of the ponies, but although it gave her a shock and put her out of action for the afternoon (on account of not being able to get her boots on) it didn't dampen her enthusiasm. I regaled her with stories of the times Kate, Em and I had been trodden on and as the tally rose I wondered how we could have been so careless...

Malcolm and I spend a lot of time arguing. These arguments are very vehement while they last but there is no malice in them and we feel that they keep us sharp and up to the mark as we grow older. The fact is that we have opposing views on many thing: politics – he's very left wing in his views while mine are a little further to the right: royalty – he's republican and I'm mildly monarchist: religion – he's a staunch Methodist while I'm a keen member of the Church of England: literature – he's devoted to the Russian writers and George Orwell while I'm a Jane Austen fan. I could go on, but at least it makes for some lively conversation. We never sit together in silence...

On one thing, though, we are in complete agreement. We just love our life at Harcombe and don't crave exotic holidays,

The valley, with Harcombe Wood on the right

though we have had a good few in the past. But we do enjoy short breaks away from home and a couple of day in London are always a joy.

This month we took the bus (an excellent way of travelling to London, and very inexpensive) to visit our friends Ada and Istvan who had booked for us all to see the Ice Age Exhibition at the British Museum. Ada (it's only me who calls her Ada, her real name is Sally) and I have known one another for more than half a century. We met on my very first day at Bristol University where we were both embarking on an undergraduate drama course, and we hit it off immediately. After we graduated our paths didn't cross for a long time, although we still kept in touch, but when we met again I remembered what it was that had made us such good friends. We have totally different temperaments but exactly the same sense of humour – we remembered all the things which we had laughed at all those years ago and we still found them funny, although I doubt than anyone else did. It was through Ada that I met Heather who has been one of my closest friends ever since. And we love Ada's husband Istvan, a very anglicised Hungarian.

It's always exciting when the bus gets to London and we see the city in all its glory (it wasn't raining that day). As we rumble along the Embankment, past posh Cheyne Walk, with the Thames on the other side, and then turn towards Chelsea Hospital and Sloane Square, Malcolm and I (we in are complete agreement on this one) feel very proud to be English. We treat ourselves to a taxi ride to the British Museum, partly because we hate struggling on the underground but mainly because we never tire of travelling through London and passing the sights we have seen so many times before.

The exhibition was fascinating and there followed the usual convivial evening with Ada and Istvan in their delightful house in Muswell Hill. The next day we were particularly proud of ourselves since we did manage to travel from Highgate to Victoria to catch the coach home, on the tube, without going wrong once. Nor did we have to deal with the mysteries of the ticket machines since there was always someone on hand to help us, and a cheerful someone at that. It always used to be said that Londoners were unfriendly and unhelpful. Maybe they were, but not any more. And, of course, it helps if you are elderly and look confused and helpless... We're pretty good at that.

It was a great couple of days doing things we don't usually do but, as ever, it was good to be back at Harcombe again.

Ruby, when Em asked her what she would like to do best on her seventh birthday, replied that she wanted to have it at Harcombe. This brought a small tear to my eye when I considered all the options open to a child today. It's good to know how much the grandchildren love coming here, not to mention all the "adopted grandchildren" who come each weekend to ride and, I think, consider the farm a second home. School had started but the birthday was on a Saturday, so down they came again.

The party was a great success. The guests ranged from Janine who is a few years younger than me, has been like a fairy godmother to Kate and Em since they were tiny, and is another adopted member of our family, to Amelia, aged four. Amelia adores her bigger cousins and loves it when they are here. Much pizza was eaten and Em, as always, had concocted a cake in what seemed like about ten minutes and which was so delicious that it was almost all consumed. Em's efforts put mine of many years ago to shame. The choice then was between a gingerbread house with liquorice allsorts for windows and doors or a caterpillar, made with ginger biscuits stuck together with cream and with jelly tots for eyes and nose. Neither required much culinary skill. I do notice, though, that the date brownie which later formed the basis for so many teenage birthday cakes still features large in Em's repertoire.

And the day, April 20, was hot enough for June.

In the meantime, I had almost poisoned Gypsy by giving her one of the pills meant for Charlie instead of the ones she was taking for an ongoing ear infection. Charlie has a condition called Cushings' Disease which is common in old horses and is on permanent medication which works very well. It isn't good for dogs, though, and my mistake made a Saturday morning visit to the vet very necessary. They kept her for a few hours, made her vomit, and sent her home with some liquid charcoal in two glass bottles which I was supposed to mix with her meals. She didn't get much of it in the end because I dropped one of the bottles on the tiled kitchen floor and spent quite some time cleaning up the black liquid, mixed with broken glass, both of which had contrived to spread themselves over a wide area. Gypsy soon recovered and was back to her cheerful, unapologetic, food-thieving self.

The rather shaming thing was that it wasn't the first time that I had made a mistake with Charlie's pills, only that time I nearly poisoned Malcolm. On this particular day he ate his breakfast and then started vomiting. When he turned grey and his forehead got clammy I made him go back to bed and then called the doctor. Malcolm hadn't been visited at home by the doctor for thirty years but he felt too ill to protest. After various tests the doctor confessed that he had no idea what had caused the vomiting but it was possibly a bug or something he had eaten. He gave him an injection and left, advising us not to mix with other people for a day or two in case we were harbouring something infectious.

Sometime later the patient began to feel a lot better and came down for a lightly poached egg. I then had occasion to go to my handbag and it became all too clear what the cause of the sickness had been. The previous day I had called at the pharmacy for Malcolm's blood pressure pills. I had then gone to the vet for Charlie's Cushing's Disease pills. And as Malcolm's pills were still in my handbag it didn't take long for the penny to drop. No wonder he had been so ill... I couldn't bring myself to confess to the doctor but I telephoned NHS Direct and the nice ladies who give advice, once they had stopped laughing, decided that no lasting harm had been done.

As for Malcolm, he declared it had been well worth feeling so ill to have such a cracking story to dine out on in the future.

Which he has certainly done. But I really must be more careful. It's a funny story but what if I hadn't discovered my mistake and he had, to coin a phrase, gone on taking the pills?

Sadly this month, Malcolm lost three elderly members of his family. His cousin Aubrey was the first, closely followed by Auntie Nora, a great favourite of mine – a real Lancashire woman who saw life as it was. She was 95 and the funeral near Lancaster, which Anne, Malcolm and I went to, was a celebration of a life well lived, in a church filled with family and friends. I shall miss her, though.

We returned to the news that Cousin Jessie had died, aged 92, after a short spell in hospital. Cousin Jessie was something else. Less than five feet tall, in her prime she could shear a sheep as fast as her big hefty cousins and, in her capacity as a midwife, she had delivered many of the younger members of her family. But most of all, she was a very saintly person. She never had to bang on about her Christian faith. She lived it, but with the best sense of humour and capacity for fun and adventure that any of us ever knew. She was a joy to know and she made the best marmalade I ever tasted. What a gap she has left.

Now, as the month draws to a close, there are more signs of spring. The leaves of bluebells and wild garlic are carpeting Harcombe Wood – no flowers yet, though. There are buds on the beech trees and the rooks have built their untidy, precarious nests. The grass is beginning to grow, the blackthorn is actually in flower and the cherry tree is a picture.

Let's see what May brings.

Hooray! Hooray The first of May!
Outdoor sex begins today!

Anon (perhaps luckily)

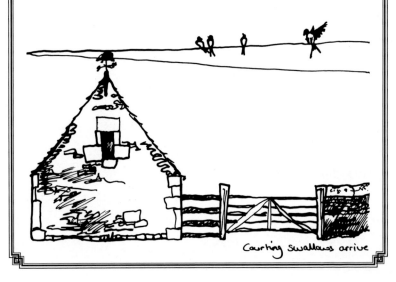

Courting swallows arrive

May

So goes the old country saying. But it would have been a brave – or desperate – lover and his lass who would have risked the downpour which lasted for the whole of May Day for a bit of hey nonny nonny in a soaking wet field or wood. Brave singers stood on top of church towers to welcome in the May and village schools hastily moved their maypoles indoors for their dancing displays. It was a washout.

Things improved, however, for the holiday weekend. The sun shone, the sky was blue, with fluffy clouds floating across it, people got in their cars and headed for the nearest coast, forgetting how much water had come down from the sky only two days earlier. The Sunday papers had pictures of people bathing and eating ice creams – the sort of things you would expect them to do on a May Bank Holiday – only this year it was big news. And, optimists as we Brits are, we felt that summer was on its way.

We were wrong of course. Down came the rain again or if not the rain, then a cold wind blew. Casting clouts was simply not an option. Spring is coming but it's certainly taking its time. The grass is growing but very slowly and the arable crops are still way behind for the time of year. Even I, the eternal optimist, began to believe the dire forebodings of the weather forecasters and the farming community.

Then the swallows arrived. Not as many as usual had made it back from Africa this year but they had returned to Harcombe as they have done for as long as Malcolm can remember. It always lifts our hearts to see them wheeling and diving through the air and lining up on the electric wires, singing fit to burst their tiny lungs. One swallow does not make a summer but this year, after they arrived, the first real signs of growth began to show. Walking Gypsy, I saw green leaves appearing in Harcombe Wood and the oil seed rape growing at last in the field which, for obvious reasons, we call Sixty Acres. Cowslips bloomed on the steep banks of the ponies' fields and the smell of bluebells wafted in the breeze. Not before time, spring was upon us at last, though the nights were still cold and the days not up to the average for the time of year.

At the same time as the swallows a little black cat appeared on the farm and did not seem keen to leave in spite of Gypsy (who lives very amicably with our three cats) chasing him at every opportunity. It was his voice which originally drew our attention to him – a loud, eery cry which echoed through the dark garden. At first he spent the nights under a thick hedge, ravenously gulping down the food I put out for him, then he ventured into the back porch and curled up on the blanket I had left in the hope that he would find it. It was more than obvious that he was an entire tom cat but he certainly didn't behave like one, purring loudly whenever we picked him up, rubbing round our legs and jumping on to Malcolm's knee when he saw him sitting down. By this time, of course, he had ventured into the house and seemed disinclined to leave. Malcolm took to him instantly, just as he had to Crocodile, the tiny stray kitten which he had rescued after it had fallen down the shaft of a grain elevator on the farm and who had died at the ripe old age of 16 only last year. It wasn't too fanciful to feel that the little black cat had arrived to replace him.

But he was so delightful that my conscience began to prick me as I thought of the family who might be searching for their much loved pet. I rang the local cattery and Alan, whom I know well since all our cats – except Croc – have come from him, told me that no one was looking for a lost black tomcat. He advised me to take him to the vet, get him checked for a microchip and, if there wasn't one, to have him neutered and to keep him if that was what we wanted – which, of course, it was. The cat was perfectly happy to be put in a cat basket and very well behaved as Rebecca ran her scanner over him. No sign of a chip – what a relief... He was relieved of his manhood and came back to join the Harcombe gang. My conscience no longer troubled me although his appearance remains a complete mystery.

It was Hazel who christened him Baggie which is not short

for Bag Puss but for Bagheera, the handsome black panther with the large green eyes, the friend of Ballou the bear in Kipling's Jungle Book. It suits him perfectly. He is now well established at Harcombe and he and Gypsy have settled their differences to such an extent that he now comes with us on many of our walks. If she becomes too over excited towards him, he gives her a bang on the nose which soon sorts her out.

Although I never want to live anywhere else than Harcombe, it's a lot of fun to go and visit either Kate or Emily from time to time. They live such different lives from me and I love sharing those lives occasionally. Also, because we have far too many material things, Kate usually gives me London experiences for birthday and Christmas presents. This time it was a late Christmas present and she had booked tickets for a play called 'Peter and Alice' starring up-and-coming young actor Ben Wishaw and the incomparable Dame Judi Dench. The play was about a fictitious meeting between Peter Llewellyn-Jones, whom J M Barrie used as his model for Peter Pan and Alice Liddell who was Lewis Carroll's muse for Alice in Wonderland, and how it had affected their lives. There was no interval, no chance to break the magic, for magic it was, and at the end the cast had a standing ovation. Then out for a meal in Covent Garden, back to stay for the first time in Kate and Simon's new house, shopping in Oxford Street the next day and home on the coach with my head still full of Peter and Alice. Wonderful to go away but lovely to be home again.

I had a birthday experience this month as well, although

my birthday isn't until June. This was a trip, organised by Liz, to Swindon Literary Festival to hear Clare Balding, television sports commentator and all round good egg, speaking about her bestselling book, 'My Animals and Other Family'. Clare is even better in the flesh than on the television and we had a great evening, coming home with a copy of her book which I couldn't put down until I'd finished it. I didn't get a chance even to open it that evening, though, because when I got home I found Malcolm with a bloody nose, injured hand and bruised knee. He had gone up the road to look at a spectacular sky, heard a noise in the wood, jumped up the bank to see what it was, got his foot caught in a bramble and fallen into the road. Luckily his rather large nose (which he doesn't always think of as an advantage) hit the tarmac before his head but it wasn't a pretty sight, even when cleaned up.

A visit to A&E the following day revealed a tiny broken bone in his hand and a later visit to the doctor was necessary due to a still swollen knee. The delightful staff at Cirencester Hospital are on Christian name terms with my accident-prone husband whose cheerful banter appears to brighten up their day. "Hello Malcolm," they say when he appears – again – "what have you done this time?"

The weather was even better for the Spring Bank Holiday at the end of the month and a great treat for all of us was the arrival of my stepson, Ross, accompanied by his lovely girlfriend Jess and with adventure on his mind. I first met Ross when he was a skinny, bespectacled little boy of 11 but we had an adventure together that very first day. When paddling in the sea at Westward Ho! (in wellingtons and fully clothed because it was February) I shouted to him to jump from the rock he was standing on and I would give him a piggy-back to the beach. Somehow we both misjudged it and landed in the freezing water. Ross looked terrified until I burst out laughing and it was the beginning of a very loving and lasting friendship. Luckily we were due to visit some friends who lived nearby and were able to borrow a change of clothes...

Ross, now in his late thirties, tall and very fit, is into extreme sports in a big way and the one he wanted to try this Bank Holiday weekend was the annual Cheese Rolling at Cooper's Hill, near Brockworth, on the edge of Gloucester. This has taken place allegedly since the fifteenth century and one theory – I really like this one – is that the villagers were trying to arrest the sun to ensure that there would be summer sunlight all the year round. The sun was represented by a large Double Gloucester cheese being rolled down the one in three gradient followed by a crowd of young men all trying to catch it.

In 2010, because this somewhat bizarre event was attracting huge crowds of people from all over the world (many of whom had read about it on the internet) the local council announced plans for extra security, perimeter fencing and special spectator areas on the grounds of health and safety, that modern killer of all things that are even a tiny bit adventurous. The folk of Brockworth, however, weren't going to be told what they could or couldn't do and staged the event with none of these regulations, with no management committee and no paramedics. Human nature being what it is, even more people travelled from the far corners of the world to try their luck or simply to watch the spectacle. The police closed all roads to Cooper's Hill but it simply increased people's determination and they were prepared to walk the distance to get there. On that first 'illegal' running of the race, 500 people turned up and there were no major accidents or unacceptable behaviour.

On this particular Bank Holiday morning, Ross and Jess set off early and Emily, Daisy, Ruby and I followed later, parking the car in the farmyard of our friend Derek and puffing up the steep track to see the fun – if fun it turned out to be. Ross seemed unconcerned but Em and I were terrified for his safety. Cooper's

There were one or two other spectators at the finish...

Hill looked even steeper the closer we got to it and my pride at being one of the oldest people to have done the initial climb began to evaporate. But although he had one fall and didn't win the cheese, Ross acquitted himself well and charged down to the bottom into a row a hefty rugby players who were forming a human barrier. The camera he was wearing on his head (until he fell) took some spectacular photographs which he posted on Facebook the following day and which then, as they say, went global. There was also footage of the race on the national news where we could easily spot Ross in his bright green tee-shirt...

Against the odds, it was a real fun day out. Crowd numbers must at least have doubled since 2010 but everyone was incredibly friendly and obviously enjoying themselves as much as we were. We came home and opened a bottle of champagne, provided by a relieved Emily.

In a normal May we would have put in our bedding plants earlier in the month but we daren't risk it after a trip to the local nursery and a warning from the people who run it that we should wait until there was no risk of frost. And we believed them.

Although I'm quite happy fiddling about with bedding plants, I actually hate gardening. I know that I should like it – most people do, or say they do – but I find it terribly tedious and keep thinking of things that I would rather be doing. Honestly, I'd as soon clean the house and I'd certainly prefer to muck out the stables – which is perhaps just as well as I have to do that every day.

Ross on a roll

Even when I was a teenager I used to chuckle when my parents were, as I put it, scratching around in the garden. Then, during the early years of my first marriage, we bought a derelict farm house surrounded by three acres of similarly neglected garden and that was really when the rot set in. It wasn't called Quarry Farm for nothing – I swear there were more stones than soil and they never seemed to get less, however many we chucked over the wall into the adjoining field. But Brian, my first husband, was nothing if not tenacious, and we grew all manner of stuff, mainly vegetables and soft fruit which it was my job to pick, freeze or give away to anyone who would accept our generous bounty. It was lovely to have so much fruit and veg, particularly as we had very little money, having spent most of what we had on the house, but there is a limit. Kate and Em have never managed to stomach gooseberries since the day we left Quarry Farm and I still have a vivid image of all the green and slimy caterpillars that we used to pick off the cabbages before we ate them – or gave them away.

Eventually we moved to a small converted barn with a postage stamp of a garden and lots of room for flower pots and tubs. That really was my kind of gardening and it was one May evening when I was bending inelegantly over a large pottery sink, planting geraniums, that Malcolm arrived to ask me out for the very first time. That was more than twenty years ago and, ever the romantic, he has planted out the borders at Harcombe with geraniums ever since. I still have my pots, tubs and sinks filled with bright bedding plants which need very little attention once I have put them in and until this year I have always had lots in the stable yard too. However, I have now opted for hanging baskets in the yard, much to Lorna's relief, since they are safe from the attentions of her goats.

There's a big area of grass in the garden and at one time Malcolm did all the mowing. But there are three bits of lawn on different levels and it's really hard work to lug the mower from one to another. Once again, Brian and Cathy have come to the rescue and do a grand job of lawns, verges and other bits of grass which have never seen a mower before. Whatever should we do without them?

The vegetable garden at Harcombe is not on the scale of the one I laboured in, just across the valley, at Quarry Farm. In fact, we only grow broad beans, to which Malcolm is addicted, and a few runners to keep us going when the broad beans are over. In past years Malcolm has battled with predators such as slugs, mice and pigeons but at last he has devised a scheme which seems to have foiled them all. He grows the broad bean plants to a reasonable size in large plastic tubs and then we plant them out in far from straight rows. I say 'we' but actually I mean me, on my hands and knees, because Malcolm is too stiff to kneel down and I'm beginning to feel that I might be getting that way too. Anyway, there's an excellent 'Pick-Your-Own' at the bottom of Birdlip Hill...

We have finally got all the plants in, much to my relief because now I can relax and enjoy the summer – if we ever get one.

It's the end of May, and still no clouts cast. Will it be flaming June? I wonder.

The arching boughs unite between
The columns of the temple green...
Annihilating all that's made
To a green though in a green shade.

Andrew Marvell ~ *The Garden*

Beech trees in Harcombe Wood

June

_____

At last, at last summer is here and Andrew Marvell's words, written more than three centuries ago are as true today as they were then. Especially in Harcombe Wood where the enormous beech trees form a canopy of such beauty that it rivals the medieval stone vaulting in Gloucester Cathedral. Now everything around us is green – everything, that is, except for the wild garlic which grows like a carpet of starry white flowers all over the wood. When the early evening sun shines through the trees and they cast their long shadows against the bright light, it is a truly magical sight which Gypsy and I are privileged to enjoy on every sunny day at this time of year.

I took my cousin Claire for a walk through the wood, knowing that she would be as captivated as I always am, and she was. It reminded me of the time when she was ten and I was twenty and we went looking for shells on the shoreline of the northern seaside town where I was born and brought up. I'll always remember the look of wonder on her face as we picked out the shells from the seaweed and it was there again, half a century later as the sunbeams shone in Harcombe Wood.

It has not been sunny every day, though, it's still cold at night and often in the daytime too. And wet, but not as bad as last month. But there has been just enough warmth to make the hedgerows green and for wild flowers to bloom in the verges which are now glowing with blue cranesbill, pink campion, lacy white cow parsley, bobbing dog daisies, wild forget-me-nots and clover . When I minded Amelia while Liz went riding, we went looking for wild flowers and even I was surprised at the number of different species we found just walking down Harcombe Valley. She's still little enough to want to pick only the heads but enough survived until we got back and wrote down their names and colours for her to take home and, hopefully, remember a few. We treated nettle stings with dock leaves and sucked the honey out of clover flowers – just as I did when walking with my grandparents and as Kate and Em did with theirs.

This month Malcolm and I have been on rather too frequent rabbit duty due to Pumpkin's insatiable instinct to catch baby rabbits and bring them in, live, to show us. Pumpkin lives here on the farm with us but belongs to Daisy and, of all the cats I have ever owned (a lot) he is, in most respects, the perfect pet for a child. Black and white, fluffy and incredibly laid back, he lounges around the house, sleeping on beds, sofas or the chair you particularly wanted to sit on, purring loudly and refusing to move. He will sit on Daisy's knee for as long as she wants him to. But as the young rabbits begin to multiply in their warrens at the top of the valley, he takes on a new persona.

When Daisy was about five, I found her walking around with Pumpkin, quite uncomplaining, tucked under her arm. "Has he hurt his leg, darling?" I enquired. "Oh no, Gran, but you said he kept catching baby rabbits and if I've got hold of him, he can't do that can he?" was the reply. The trouble is, Daisy can't watch him all the time and neither can we, so not infrequently, in the early morning we hear a Pumpkin hunting cry and a lot of scuffling round the bedroom. Although we try at first to ignore it we know that Mr P has come rushing up the plank and through the cat flap in the bedroom window, rabbit in mouth, and then felt compelled to let it go, just for the fun of catching it again. He never learns that, once a baby rabbit is let loose in a room full of furniture, there's very little chance that he will succeed.

That means that it's up to Malcolm and me to find the rabbit and set it free. But it's not the easiest thing in the world for two elderly people, just wakened from sleep, to go crawling about the floor hunting baby rabbits which usually, sensibly, run under the bed or a very heavy chest of drawers. Malcolm's reactions are much quicker than mine but I'm marginally more agile and slightly less likely to be unable to get up from the floor with rabbit in hand, as has happened more than once. The next task is to return young Peter to his natural habitat and, if anyone is abroad that early, they could witness the bizarre sight of an elderly woman in spotted dressing gown and wellingtons,

Pumpkin doesn't find it so easy to catch Rabbits when Daisy is here

legging it up the road and down the valley to where we hope he lives. Having read Watership Down, I have great faith in the good sense of rabbits but they really must look out for Pumpkin's approach and get their young back to the burrow – after all, he's not hard to spot.

My birthday falls on midsummer day which is not the 21st of June as many people think (that's the longest day) but the 24th. In my mind's eye I see childhood birthdays when the sun always shone but in reality there were many times when my mother had to run in from birthday tea in the garden, carrying a rain-bespattered cake which we would then eat indoors. This year, after all the rain and cold weather, I struck lucky and my birthday was warm and sunny. Malcolm asked me what I wanted to do and, because I had had a big birthday celebration last year, I opted to stay at home and get our supper from a wonderful shop in Cheltenham where you can buy superb food from the freezer. We didn't exactly have a quiet day because several people called with cards and presents, including Chris and Johnny who stayed for lunch, the phone rang constantly and it was just before closing time when we finally collected our sea bass and luxury ice cream from the shop. It was warm enough to enjoy a glass of wine on the balcony, looking out across the farm, and feeling that summer had really come at last.

And for the next few days it seemed that it had and that it would be a fine evening for the surprise treat that Anne, Chris and Johnny had arranged as my birthday present. The rain which began to fall heavily just as we were setting off was not forecast and they began to get a bit depressed as we drove through winding country lanes to a secret destination. This turned out to be Belas Knap, a prehistoric burial barrow, high on the Cotswolds near the historic town of Winchcombe, but the rain was still falling and we had a short walk to reach the barrow. No one seemed keen to get out of the car but, with an astonishing piece of luck, we managed to drive up a farm lane to find Belas Knap in full view only a short distance away. We sat in the car and drank champagne which Chris had brought and, in true British style, decided that we were having the greatest fun – which indeed, we were. Then on to a meal at one of our favourite pubs, famed for its jump racing connections and its asparagus (which we all sampled) and home after a very successful, if damp, evening.

The month ended with a lovely surprise – a visit from Miss Daisy, on her own for the first time. Daisy and Ruby have been several times without Em but I did wonder if she would miss her volatile little sister when she went to bed. Not a bit of it. Daisy spent the whole weekend with a permanent smile on her face. She went for a long ride with 'the big girls' who took her down to the lakes in Miserden Park, a spectacularly beautiful place, and then had a barbecue on the balcony with Malcolm and me, which included a plateful of one of her favourite foods – Malcpa's chips. We let her stay up a bit later than usual and she went to bed very happily, getting up the next morning to set the breakfast table and make cups of tea and coffee for us, as she always does.

She decided that, instead of riding that day, she would lunge William. I wasn't too sure about this as I hate lunging – it makes me feel dizzy as the horse, on a long rein, goes round and round me in circles. Daisy was adamant that she knew what to do, because her friend Emily had shown her, and she isn't the sort of child who will say she can do something unless she is sure. Off we went to the little paddock which is one of the few flat places on the farm and she soon had William trotting and cantering round her in a way that even the Pony Club would approve of. I just love the way she has taken to the pony scene and I'm sure

Ruby always finds herself having an adventure when she visits

it's because we've never tried to force her into it. William, of course, is the icing on the cake. She just adores him.

When Em and Ruby arrived for lunch and to collect her, it was obvious that the visit had been a huge success. It gets harder and harder to part with them when they leave. How I envy grandparents whose grandchildren live nearby.

In spite of the fun we've had, this month has been enormously clouded by Louise being rushed into hospital with a brain haemorrhage. Luckily she was able to go to Frenchay Hospital, near Bristol, which is the best in the country for any problems connected with the head and brain. I had daily reports from her sister Charlotte and to begin with her situation didn't look good. Every small improvement seemed to be followed by a setback but at last she began to rally and was able, in a low-key way, to enjoy her 50th birthday, albeit while still in hospital.

Louise and I have been friends for more than a quarter of a century. Our friendship started with horses and continued with horses and riding but it became more than that and, in spite of the age difference of nearly twenty years, it is a very precious friendship in many ways. I like to think that during the long time that Bradley, Louise's husband, had cancer from which he eventually died, Harcombe provided a small sanctuary where she could temporarily put her problems to one side and enjoy herself. Certainly she brightened many a day for us. All the time that she was ill – with no guarantee that she would recover – I thought of all the fun and all the laughs we had had together and I kept finding things that she had given me or bought for one of the ponies, usually Charlie, who she loves almost as much as I do. I just couldn't believe that those times might be gone forever.

Then I had a call from Charlotte to say that she was soon to leave hospital, followed by another call from Steve, her boyfriend, to say that she was home. But the best news of all was when I rang to see how she getting on and she answered the phone herself. We chatted as if she had never been ill; she obviously has a long way to go yet but the old Louise was certainly there on the end of the telephone. That was one of the best moments of this year, never mind this month.

And willows, willow herb and grass,
And meadowsweet and haycocks dry,
No whit less still and lonely fair
Than the high cloudlets in the sky.

Edward Thomas ~ *Adlestrop*

Willow and willow herb in the verge

July

Edward Thomas wrote those evocative words in the summer of 1914, late June to be exact, just before the world went mad. The train taking him to Dymock on the north western edge of Gloucestershire to see his fellow poet and friend Robert Frost, stopped briefly at the tiny station in the Oxfordshire village of Adlestrop which he immortalised forever in his sixteen line poem. The station has long been closed and you can't even get onto the platform any more but the surrounding landscape remains much the same as it was a century ago.

This June when, in spite of an upturn in the weather, the landscape remained decidedly damp, it was not until July that the farmers got round to making the modern version of "haycocks dry" – in other words, huge round or oblong bales which are now, briefly, a rather dramatic part of the landscape.

Flaming June it wasn't, but July more than made up for it. Day after day of sunshine, tractors working every daylight hour and beyond to get in the hay crop the farmers had once despaired of, the field behind the farm aglow with dog daisies, wild scabious, purple knapweed and pink clover, baby swallows emerging from their nests to perch precariously on the electric wires and to practise their flying skills before making the perilous journey to Africa for the winter. I saw more butterflies than I have seen for years. What a wonderful, unpredictable country this is!

The weather forecasters began to change their predictions about this being the wettest summer on record as people swapped wellies, waterproofs and sweaters for shorts, tee-shirts and less. The smell of barbecued food hung on the air and we enjoyed a glass of wine on our balcony more often than in the last five years. The continuous sunshine acted like a tonic – everybody looked better and felt better as they went about their business and enjoyed their leisure time outside.

Deer love the field of wildflowers behind the farmhouse

At Harcombe we all made the most of this welcome turnaround. But there was a downside. Almost every summer we are plagued by vicious horse flies which not only bite the horses but the humans as well. I wouldn't mind so much if it wasn't for the fact that, like everyone else, human and animal, they seem to want to make their home on the farm. If we walk or ride half a mile up the lane in either direction, they disappear, only to descend again when we return. In fact, riding is somewhat curtailed during the horse fly season and the horses spend most of their days either in the stable or swathed in netting rugs and masks which must present an odd sight to walkers who pass by. In my innocence and optimism, I thought that the harsh winter might have killed off these nasty creatures but, in fact, they appeared later and stayed well into August. Never mind, at least the sun was shining.

This hot July weather and the fact that Louise is very much in my thoughts at the moment, reminds me of a bizarre incident at Harcombe (no shortage of those) which took place a few years ago.

Lorna had mentioned to me that her horses and Peta's, which at the time were grazing in the Lynches at the far end of the farm, were not drinking the water from the stream which runs through the field and she wondered if a dead pheasant might be polluting the water. This stream emerges from the ground and goes into a covered stone trough and then into a smaller open trough before flowing on into the little lake which Malcolm and his family created more than thirty years ago. I understood

Lorna to say that she thought the pheasant might be in the open trough and passed this information on to Malcolm. Never being one to put things off, he and Louise – I was at work and she had come to deal with the horses – went down on the tractor to see what was going on. They found no corpse in the water and Malcolm declared, "Lorna must be on the magic mushrooms, there's nothing here." Then, always being one to make the dramatic gesture, he scooped up some water in his hand and drank it. He did admit that it tasted rather peculiar and that the taste remained with him for the rest of the day...

Speaking to Lorna later, he ascertained that I had given him duff information and that she suspected that whatever had died had done so in the covered trough, not the open one. Next morning he and Louise set out again. They lifted the lid off the trough and a horrific sight met their eyes. The body of a young sheep which had obviously been there for some time, had disintegrated in the trough. The smell was awful and when Malcolm tried to get it out with a long handled fork it dissolved into a soup-like consistency. Louise fled off to vomit in one direction and Malcolm in the other. Finally, with handkerchiefs to their faces, they managed to clear the trough and make sure that fresh water was beginning to flow through. Malcolm's main thought, not surprisingly, was that he had drunk the polluted water the previous day. His sense of the dramatic had really kicked in by the time he and Louise got back to the farm where, luckily, the first person they saw was Lesley Pollock.

The Pollocks, Lesley, Derek and their daughter, Susie, are

very good friends who for many years have brought their horses to graze at Harcombe during the summer and to enjoy the marvellous riding in Miserden Park. Susie was the very first of the 'horsey' girls to come riding with me, long before I came to Harcombe and we have been friends ever since. We just love it when, like the swallows, the Pollocks return every year. That day Lesley had come to check on the horses. More importantly, Lesley is a nurse and Malcolm blurted out to her the details of his latest escapade. She looked at him, eyes twinkling, and said in her soft Irish voice, "Well, Malcolm, you're still alive and you're a farm boy. I think you'll be all right." And he was.

Malcolm and his brother Johnny have had many adventures, most involving a tractor

The stream flowed with fresh water again and the horses started drinking but who put the body of a dead sheep into the trough and closed the lid, remains forever a mystery.

Louise has rescued Malcolm from some strange predicaments; in fact, there was a time when it was an enormous relief to me, when I was at work, to know that she was often at the farm to keep an eye on him. It was lucky that they both went off down Harcombe Valley together on the morning when he had decided to spray a particularly dense patch of nettles. When they reached the spot he heaved the knapsack sprayer, heavy with nettle killer, onto his back and Louise set off to check the horses which were further down the valley. When she returned she found Malcolm lying on his back in the nettles, looking like a stranded turtle. He had managed to trip over and, due to the weight of the sprayer, had fallen backwards and been unable to move. She heaved him up and, although quite badly stung, he finished the job. We now get someone to cut down the nettles each year...

Because the weather has turned so warm and dry we water the garden most days. I don't mind doing this, it's not like proper gardening. One Saturday morning I was sloshing water on what was by now a fine display of geraniums when I became aware that I wasn't on my own. On the other side of the garden wall was a young couple who asked me if there was a right of way where they could walk with a group of Italian teenagers whose coach taking them on a visit to Gloucester Cathedral had broken down on the main road. It would take at least an hour to get a replacement coach to take them on their way.

I persuaded them that they would all be more comfortable eating their packed lunches in our shady garden or roaming about the farm if they were intent on taking exercise. Malcolm, of course, when he heard what had happened, was even more insistent that they should stay with us until they were able to go on their way. He loves the farm to be enjoyed by as many people as possible and is far from the image (often all too accurate) of the irate, red faced farmer shaking his fist and shouting "Get off my land!"

The replacement coach took much longer than predicted to arrive and so the group of around thirty youngsters and several leaders spent a happy afternoon on the farm, running up and down the valley, admiring the ponies (Charlie was particularly glad to oblige) and generally enjoying themselves. I really like Italians – maybe it's the climate that makes them so good natured – and we had a lot of fun with them. Photographs were taken and email addresses exchanged. Finally their transport arrived and off they went to Gloucester where they especially wanted to see the tomb of Edward II who suffered a grisly death in Berkeley Castle. They sent us a delightful thank you letter but we rather felt that we should thank them for giving us such an unusual and jolly afternoon.

The British, as can be seen from our enjoyment of my birthday visit to Belas Knap last month, can always make the best of things, particularly the weather. But, my goodness, it's nice not to have to and this July we almost began to take day after day of sunshine for granted. It was so hot during the Harcombe Society's outing to literary Tewkesbury that we were rather relieved to cool off in the town's magnificent medieval abbey and to take a trip up the river in a boat with a sun canopy. While in the Abbey Malcolm pointed out the tomb of the Duke of Clarence, ill-fated (as were most of his relations) brother of Richard III. According to Shakespeare, Clarence was terrified of water and here were his mortal remains entombed in a building at the confluence of two great rivers, the Severn and the Avon, where the vaults were frequently flooded...

We also took in Abel Fletcher's Mill, so called because it features in 'John Halifax, Gentleman' by Mrs Craik, a lesser known woman novelist of the nineteenth century, set mainly in the town. We had coffee at the Royal Hop Pole Hotel where Mr Pickwick and his friends had rather too much to drink in Dickens' Pickwick Papers and passed the splendid black and white Tudor House, the home of twentieth century writer and naturalist John Moore, most of whose novels centre round Tewkesbury and the surrounding villages. A museum of natural history in some old almshouses near the Abbey is a lasting memorial to him, even if his books don't appeal. All in all a grand day out.

I hardly dared hope the warm spell would last for my next trip to London but ten days later I boarded the coach for the capital wearing thin linen trousers and a tee-shirt – and was glad of the air conditioning. The occasion was a rather delayed treat for a milestone birthday that I actually celebrated last year and I was on my way to Kate and Simon's house while Em, Daisy and Ruby travelled from the north so that we could all spent the weekend together. The girls had booked a trip down the Thames, followed by another on the London Eye and it was fascinating to see all the landmarks, first from the river and then, so to speak, from the air. Having indulged ourselves between trips at a noodle house on the South Bank we returned to the Eye to find a huge queue and would have aborted our mission if we had not been assured by one of the official queue controllers that it would only take 40 minutes. She was right and we passed the time taking turns in the queue and making friends with the cosmopolitan crowd who were waiting. It was all very orderly and quite added to the occasion. Then home to Kate and Simon's for a barbecue after another grand day out and a great birthday treat.

I got home and immediately started to prepare for a visit from our American friends Jim and Gena. Malcolm got to know Gena many years ago when she was secretary to the American Ambassador in London and her husband Jim, a juvenile judge in Massachusetts, is just the sort of person you would want to appear before if you were a young offender in need of help. We love them dearly and we hadn't seen them since we met in Ireland several years ago so we had a lot to catch up on.

Because Jim's family come from Ireland it seemed a good occasion to take them to meet Michael and Davnet McGinty whom we had met under the most bizarre circumstances nearly twenty years ago on a trip to Moscow. We were standing in

Moscow airport which seemed to be inhabited mainly by prostitutes and armed guards in important looking uniforms. When our courier, who was calling out our names, came to McGinty, Malcolm rather unwisely started singing Paddy McGinty's Goat, which at the time did not go down well with his namesakes. If looks could have killed... But, in fact, they soon forgave him and it was the start of a friendship which has stood the test of time.

We hadn't seen them since they moved to Abbotsbury, an idyllic village on the Dorset coast and the six of us spent a great weekend together, which ended in us eating oysters and drinking champagne in the garden of a restaurant overlooking Chesil Beach. Life can't get much better than that.

The end of July was the hottest that I can remember, the only rain falling on our journey to Dorset. School's out and Young Emily, Maddi, Chloe and Molly, and Eliza too, now she's home from university, are appearing most days to ride and to help me with the ponies. My thoughts are now turning to one of the main events of the Harcombe year – the Syde Pony Club Camp which I first organised in August six years ago for kids like I once was, who don't have their own ponies and would find themselves set aside at the official Pony Club. I only meant it as a one off but they all left saying "See you next year..." and I've been doing it ever since. It's incredibly hard work but I love it.

The yard gets quite full when all the girls are here

It's awfully hard luck on Diana,
Her ponies have swallowed their bits;
She fished down their throats with a spanner
And frightened them all into fits.

John Betjeman ~ *Hunter Trials*

Training the children

August

August has dawned, warm and sunny, and it's all systems go to make sure that the Syde Pony Club Camp runs on oiled wheels when it happens at the very end of the month. There really is nothing quite like our camp. We do not come under the umbrella cover of that august body, the British Horse Society, with which I have no issues at all, I simply do not necessarily abide by its rather stringent rules. Camp fees are less than half those of official Pony Club camps because we literally charge what it costs.

But the children and teenagers who come are well taught by qualified instructors (who are all paid), well fed, happy and, as far as can be guaranteed when large, sometimes unpredictable animals are concerned, safe. They come by invitation, with their safety helmets and body protectors and their parents understand that we will take care of them to the best of our ability. Dr Penny who lives at Syde Manor and Nurse Christine from nearby Caudle Green are both on hand in case of accident and I have a First Aid kit always handy. As for the ponies needs, our vets are on call should we need them and this year the children of two of the vets and the daughter of a veterinary assistant from the practice all came to camp – with their parents.

Our ethos is to make it fun as well as increasing knowledge of horses, riding and horse care. The kids wear tee shirts of different colours on the back of which is a logo with the words 'Have Fun at Syde Pony Camp and Learn Lots Too' designed by Lorna, whose talents appear to be endless. This just about sums up our aims and we must be succeeding because the same kids come back year after year and are joined by new riders every time.

I wouldn't like anyone to think that I have any quarrel with the official Pony Club which has branches worldwide. It does a wonderful job and for my own girls as they were growing up, the Cotswold Pony Club Camp was the highlight of their year. They competed as members of mounted games teams, entered show jumping competitions and one day events and they loved it. But they had had their own ponies from an early age and I was happy and able to do my stint as a helper. The youngsters who enjoy themselves at Harcombe may well not own a pony (in which case they borrow one of ours or I find one for them somehow), have a parent with a certain amount of equine knowledge or they may simply not have the confidence to face hordes of other children and ponies and sometimes (though these are largely a thing of the past) over-bossy instructors.

I regard our camp as somewhere where any youngster can learn about horses, enjoy riding and looking after them and not be intimidated by anyone. Sometimes I think I do this for the child I once was who did not have a pony or the opportunity to go to Pony Club but whose greatest wish (and how I wished) was that one day it might be so. It never was but now I am able to live what I missed through the children who come to us – and it gives me enormous pleasure.

I couldn't, of course, achieve any of this without Malcolm's co-operation, enthusiasm and enormous good nature. Horses are definitely not his thing but he loves to see people and especially youngsters enjoying themselves on the farm. So he puts up with every corner of the house and most of the outbuildings being crammed with kids, kit, ponies, mummies and everything else

The junior ride of the Harcombe Pony Camp are put through their paces

which goes with the wonderful world of the horse. Members of the senior ride traditionally stay with us, 'camping' in our sitting room, and Malcolm cooks chips for supper on at least one evening, endures the horse talk for as long as he can and then decamps to brother Johnny's for a bit of peace and a good night's sleep. I cannot think of any other man in the world who would do this.

I don't sleep very well in the weeks leading up to camp. My mind is full of what I have done and what there is still to do. Once I have made sure that our instructors can come, that the rosettes are ordered, the appropriate fields and the ménage belonging to the Manor are available (we have very little usable flat ground at Harcombe) and that the jumps, borrowed and our own, are all intact and in place, I ought to be able to relax but it isn't easy. I lie awake wondering if a certain pony will be suitable for the appropriate child, I count in my head the available stables and fields and try to decide how many we will be feeding at breakfast, lunch and supper each day. It's far from relaxing and not a bit like counting sheep. My main cause for concern this year was that we had eighteen riders and ponies to accommodate, more than we'd ever had before. What if it poured with rain, where would we put them all?

Before any of this happened, though, I had other worries. The granddaughter of a dear friend of ours who lives in France wanted to come to the Cotswolds with her boyfriend to ride horses and to brush up her English. I'm always sceptical about people who want to come and ride. How much experience have they had? Are they competent enough to go out riding on their own? Can they actually get a horse ready to go riding or has it always been done for them at a riding school?

As it turned out, I needn't have worried. Juliette and Charles knew exactly what they were doing – I knew they'd be fine when I saw Charles vault elegantly onto Splash from the ground – and after Young Emily had been out with them to show them where to go, they had Splash and Jessie to themselves for most of the week they were here. This had the added advantage of keeping the ponies fit for camp while some of the other girls were on holiday. They stayed with Johnny and Christine and rode with us every day and sometimes twice a day and they were a delight to have around. Their stay ended with a barbecue in magical Harcombe wood, the first we have been able to have there for several years. What a difference fine weather makes!

Camp, of course, ensures that the yard and stables get a really good tidy up at least once a year and by the time the end of August arrives everything is swept and scrubbed, hay and straw are in neat piles, feed tidily placed in named bins and the tack room looks as it never looks at any other time. I couldn't do this without my gang of Harcombe girls, Young Emily, Maddi, Chloe and Molly, joined by now by Eliza who is home from university and this year by Daisy and Ruby who are here for two whole weeks of their summer holiday. It's hard work but everyone seems to accept this as part of what camp has come to mean.

This year Young Emily and Eliza, who have always before

been in the senior ride, have been promoted to instructing the 'Tiddlers', as we call the youngest ride, putting into practice all they have learned on their college equine course. Our dear friend Amelia has agreed once again to teach the seniors, despite being in great demand by the surrounding official Pony Clubs. Young, glamorous and highly qualified, she manages to transform her pupils from passengers into real riders in an astonishingly short space of time, largely because she never asks the impossible from them and so she usually gets it.

Peta, who has kept her two horses at livery here for the last ten years, is a competent instructor of the Middle Ride, but this year, at nine o'clock on the first morning of camp, she telephoned to say that her mother was having severe chest pains and she had had to take her to hospital and wouldn't be able to come that day. No one can tell me that God wasn't looking down on Harcombe that late August morning. No sooner had Em brought me this piece of bad news than an unfamiliar horse box drove into view. By process of elimination I realised that this was Anna, the aunt of Daisy's friend, Morgan, who was bringing Morgan's pony to camp. I knew that she was a riding instructor and as she wound down the window to introduce herself, after the most perfunctory of greetings from me, I asked the vital question, "One of our instructors can't come, could you possibly take her place?" Dear Anna, she never hesitated: "Of course I will," she said and what a star she turned out to be.

As it happened, Peta couldn't make it for the rest of the week, though thankfully her mother quickly recovered, and Anna transformed the Middle Ride into a little group of competent nine and ten year olds who, on the final day, were jumping across country as if they had been doing it all their lives. Among them was Daisy, so fearful last year, now transformed as William showed her just what he could do when she gave him the right messages. And Tilly, usually lagging behind her twin sister, Katie, tackling the jumps with enthusiasm, cheered on by the rest.

We all agreed at the end that it had been the best camp ever. The sun shone every day, dispelling my fears of wet ponies and riders all crowding damply into the covered yard. As far as I could tell, there were no discordant voices and a lot of laughter. For me, it was a bonus to have, for the first time, all three of my granddaughters, Daisy, Ruby and little Amelia – the youngest member at only four and a half – revelling in the joy of horses as their mothers once did and still do.

Having Em there all the time, taking over the catering, together with Morgan's mum Rebecca, took a load off my shoulders. I always knew that everyone would be supplied with buns, drinks, sandwiches, cake, biscuits or a cooked meal at the appropriate time of day. All the mums turned up with delicious homemade cakes which we gorged on for the whole of camp. An army, it's said, marches on its stomach and the same applies to Pony Camp. On average we catered for between thirty and forty at lunchtime and sixteen in the evening.

The help I had from everybody was phenomenal. The vets came to talk about horse care and equine illness management;

farriers David and Alex spent the afternoon showing the kids the finer points of shoeing, using a more than willing Charlie as a model; Dr Penny gave instruction on first aid for humans who are involved with horses and darling Granny Jane (none of whose grandchildren were here this year, but she just loves coming) turned up to demonstrate the most efficient way of bathing a pony. On the final day, Val the Vicar took time off from administering to her nine parishes, to present the prizes. Nobody wanted anything for their time and trouble, saying what a pleasure it was to see people enjoying themselves so much, and looked amazed as I handed out flowers and bottles of wine, I was also given beautiful flowers from Em and Liz and countless bottles of wine which I also felt I didn't deserve for such a lot of fun.

After camp, came the Harcombe Farm Fun Day, when all the riders, their instruction over, took part in a treasure hunt, a gymkhana, a handy pony competition, cross country jumping and a mounted fancy dress parade, dismounting only to take their dogs into the dog show. There were bacon butties and ice creams for all, masses of rosettes and £350 was raised for the local branch of Riding for the Disabled whose members came to run the gymkhana. Perhaps the greatest delight was the appearance of Louise, who has been such a key player at all previous camps. She is making good progress after brain surgery and it was so good that she felt able to come.

All in all, a fantastically enjoyable, if entirely exhausting, few days. Next year? I expect so...

In the excitement of preparation for camp and its final happening, nature did not stand still. The harvest ripened in the continuous sunshine and the combines rolled well into the night, headlights flashing, until the crops were safely gathered in and all that remained in the fields was acres of stubble and huge bales of straw waiting to be collected. The blackberries were phenomenal – large, black, juicy and luckily very plentiful, which was just as well since they were so tasty that it was tempting to eat them all and not bring any home for pies, crumbles and the freezer.

The swallows, who we have watched since they first appeared in late spring are perching on the telephone wires, waiting for the day when they will set off once again for Africa. Will some of the little ones, who only learned to fly a few days ago, make the long and dangerous journey and come back to Harcombe again next year? I hope and pray they do.

So ends one of the sunniest and happiest Augusts I ever remember, and the icing on the cake was Em's announcement that she has finally made the decision to come back to live in Gloucestershire so that Daisy and Ruby can have the sort of childhood which she and Kate so enjoyed and she can pick up the threads of the life she left behind more than twenty years ago. How exciting is that?

While barred clouds bloom the soft dying day
And touch the stubble plains with rosy hue;
Hedge crickets sing; and now with treble soft
The red-breast whistles from a garden croft
And gathering swallows twitter in the skies.

John Keats ~ *Ode to Autumn*

Hunting the fields behind the house

September

Our swallows have gone now and I so hope they survive their journey to Africa and return safely to Harcombe next spring. And our resident robin is happily whistling around the stable yard, ignoring the cats which he knows are too well fed to do much serious hunting. He may have reckoned without Baggy, but Baggy has his eye on sterner prey and is bent on tackling the rats which have returned to the yard, now that the stubble fields, rosy hued or not, have yielded up their bounty. I think he will have his work cut out, but we'll see.

For the last decade or more September has meant the return to Cirencester of Gifford's Circus, a never-to-be-missed experience. When I was a child, living near Blackpool, the greatest treat was to be taken to Blackpool Tower Circus, a grand and glitzy spectacular on a gigantic scale. At the end the floor went down and the sea came in to create a finale which seemed more splendid as the years went by. Now, when I think about it

I can't believe how entranced I was by the sight of caged lions, tigers and elephants and captive sea-lions performing tricks which nature never intended them to perform. How times have changed. I can think of few people who would enjoy that sort of entertainment now.

Gifford's Circus could not be more different. Based on travelling circuses of the 1920s and 30s, throughout the summer months it pitches its Big Top on village greens and suitable flat fields in various places in Gloucestershire and Wiltshire. Its final stop is Stratton Meadow, on the edge of Cirencester and it's here that we usually see it. It is more than a circus, it is a superb artistic experience which appeals to young and old with no caged animals, just horses, the odd dog and a goose called Brian. The human beings present class acts from high wire performances to fire eating, juggling and amazing acrobatics – never forgetting Tweedie the clown, who endears himself to everybody by his sheer silliness. So popular has he become that he now stars in the local pantomime too. The music is great and the costumes are superb and look as if they have been freshly laundered every day.

The circus is the brainchild of Nell Gifford, a local girl made very, very good, whose ambition has always been to have her own circus. She is backed up by her husband Toti and an incredibly loyal team who return year after year to recreate the magic.

As a family we are rather proud of our links with this particularly wonderful enterprise. Kate, Liz and Em all went to primary school with the Gifford children and I knew their mother well. I also, in my rather grand sounding job as entertainments editor of the Wilts and Gloucestershire Standard, reviewed the circus from its very early days and got to know Nell, Toti and quite a few of the artistes. Malcolm and I were invited to first nights, last nights and circus open days – we loved the circus scene. And we have a permanent reminder of Gifford's in our pony Jessie, who is beautiful, unflappable and much loved around the yard. But it can't be denied that she is moody. One day she will do exactly as she is asked, the next she pretends she's never heard of what you want her to do and, even if she had, she's certainly not going to do it again. It's not hard to see why Nell and Toti were keen to find her a home away from the circus. She was called Jezabel when we got her and I just felt I had to change it, but I can sort of see how she came by it.

So when Em announced that she and the children would be back to look at suitable schools early in September and I discovered that their visit coincided with Gifford's last week on tour, I was off to the booking office at speed. As ever, it didn't disappoint and we spent a magical morning, together with Em's schoolfriend Kaz and her two children, Sammy and Georgie, who we met on the way in, spellbound by the activities of Nell, Tweedie and all the magnificent cast, not forgetting Brian the goose.

Daisy and Ruby had a rare day off school on the Monday of their visit, as Em had arranged for them to look around two of the local primary schools where they would go after Christmas. In the end they opted for Sapperton School, tiny and rural with a good Christian ethic. With less than 60 pupils, the school is only the size of one year's intake at their northern, urban school so it will be a bit of a culture shock for them. But they were greeted with such kindness and friendship by teachers and pupils alike that they now can't wait to go there, even Ruby, who previously stated that there was no way she would wear a green uniform...

The following weekend I was off to London again for another birthday treat (this time for this year's birthday), from Kate. We went to the most comprehensive exhibition to date of the work of the Lancashire industrial artist L S Lowry, at Tate Britain. I have been a devotee of the work of this most eccentric of artists since I saw a film about him at the local art college when I was at school, but I had seen few of his paintings in the original so this was an enormous treat and it didn't disappoint. As well as the paintings on show there were also great captions not only relating to Lowry and his life but also about the industrial north and his home town of Salford in particular, in the days when those dark Satanic mills, now long gone, were the lifeblood of Britain. Kate, Simon and I spent a wonderful afternoon there, although Kate was suffering the after effects of having her wisdom teeth removed earlier in the week. She declared that the exhibition was so special that it quite took her mind off her aching mouth.

It was on my way to London on the coach that I got involved in an incident which Malcolm's sister Anne said could only happen to him or me or, in this case, to both of us. He took me to the coach and I had to wait to get on because the elderly lady in front of me couldn't find her old person's coach pass (I for once was smugly holding mine in my hand) and was dropping coins from her purse in her efforts to look for it. In the end the driver let her on without the pass and we set off for London. When the coach stopped at Heathrow Airport the old lady, who was sitting just in front, turned to me in some distress and told me that, in the confusion of losing her bus pass she had left her anorak under a seat at the bus stop. Much worse, was the fact that her car key was in the pocket and she had left the car in the car park next to the bus stop.

I couldn't quite think how to help her but, aware that I must do something, I said I would telephone Malcolm and ask him to get in touch with the police who might, perhaps, send a copper who wasn't out catching criminal or busy filling in forms, to see if the anorak was still where she had left it I didn't hold out much hope of this happening but felt it was worth a try and it seemed to cheer her up a bit.

I heard no more until I rang Malcolm from Simon and Kate's house, where I was staying overnight, and he told me a story which seemed to spring straight out of the sketchbook of The Two Ronnies. After a very long wait, he had managed to get through to Cirencester Police Station and to talk to a very helpful WPC. He explained the seriousness of the situation in view of the car key being in the anorak pocket for any thief to find, the owner being old and away in London, not returning until the following night, and so on. The WPC then wanted a description of the anorak which I had ascertained was khaki. When he told her this she replied, "No, no, you've already told me about the car key." "The anorak is khaki," repeated Malcolm. "I know about the car key, what colour is the anorak?" persisted the WPC. "Look love," said Malcolm after several more such exchanges, "if you saw a soldier walking down the street, what colour would his uniform be?" Eventually the penny dropped. "Oh, you mean the anorak with the car key in the pocket is khaki," said the WPC. "That's right," said Malcolm. He just couldn't wait to repeat all this to me.

He's still telling the story to anyone he finds who hasn't heard it before but he's now able to add to it the happy ending. I spent a delightful evening and most of the next day with Kate and Simon, reading the newspaper, eating an Indian takeaway, getting up and breakfasting late and reading the paper again, having a look round the local shops – things I never do at home – until it was time to get back to Victoria Coach Station to return home. Who should I spot waiting for the same return coach as me but the old lady without the khaki anorak? Her face broke into a wide smile. "I'm so glad I've seen you," she said, "I felt I had to thank you for all your help. Your husband really saved the day." This was all news to me as Malcolm hadn't been able to get in touch with the police to find out what had happened. Apparently, a policeman had found the anorak (khaki) with the car key in the pocket, exactly where the old lady had said she had left it. There must have some identification in it because they managed to contact her and she rang her brother who lives not far away. He collected the anorak and put it in the car and the key under one of the wheels. When we got off the coach and she saw Malcolm who had come to meet me, she was full of thanks and he, needless to say, embraced her and told her how glad he was that it had all ended so well. We went with her to make sure that the key really was where her brother had said and after further thanks and hugs she drove off, leaving us feeling like a pair of Good Samaritans.

Autumn is late this year, possibly because both spring and summer were also late. The trees haven't yet begun to change colour and the hedgerow flowers are still blooming but the

The fields are still full of wildflowers

autumn fruits are ripening in profusion. The blackberries, already black and juicy at the end of August, are now weighing down the bramble bushes and it takes only minutes to pick enough for a substantial crumble. In apple orchards the branches are almost brushing the ground with the weight of fruit and everyone who has apples is dumping bags outside the doors of those who haven't. That includes us because we have only two very ancient apple trees at Harcombe and they are well past their sell by date – though our one elderly pear tree has produced some particularly delicious fruit this year. So we have been delighted to receive other people's surplus apples, most of which are now cooked and in the freezer with the peel and the very bruised windfalls going to the horses and the hens. This autumn truly is a season of mellow fruitfulness.

Talking of the hens, we have had two casualties this month. I thought that Pam and Debo were looking a bit seedy but decided it was probably the time of year and that they were going into a moult. Then I found Debo dead in the run and some days later Pam was prostrate in the doorway of the henhouse. We've had them for about four years so they aren't really old and they have been wonderful layers until just recently when only one hen seemed to be laying one enormous egg every two or three days. And it must have been one of those two because we haven't seen an egg since.

But now here's an odd thing. Ever since we've had the hens Nancy has been bullied by at least one of them, often being without a lot of feathers and sometimes limping where one of

Inseparable friends Nancy and Jessica

them had pecked at her leg. I even bought her a little knitted jacket which Lorna spotted on the internet. She wore it for a bit but was obviously highly embarrassed by being made to look different and eventually shed it behind a patch of nettles. We tried separating her from the others but she seemed more stressed by that and we put her back, only to find her pecked and miserable again. I always suspected Jessica who is big, blousy and extremely self confident but I now realise that I have done her an injustice. Ever since the demise of Pam and Debo, Nancy has flourished, she and Jessica are inseparable and both look plump and magnificently feathered. No eggs as yet, though.

Incidentally, my decision to call the hens after four of the Mitford sisters (who were all mad on chickens) misfired badly. In real life Pam was hideously bullied by Nancy, Jessica was constantly in disagreement with the others and Debo was the peacemaker. Not so in the feathered world however.

With the autumn colours came Jimbo, our grandson, himself a colourful character. Jimbo and his mum, Maggie, lived with us at Harcombe during the time that he was growing up. Like so many others whose lives have connections with Harcombe he regards it as his spiritual home and his visits are always a delight.

When I first knew him, Jimbo (he was called Jamie in those days) was a rather sad little boy who found it hard to make friends and, because I liked him and felt so sorry for him we would go for long walks on the farm together and later discuss the merits of the latest Harry Potter book. But sometime in his early teens (I can't pinpoint the exact time) he underwent a complete metamorphosis and became one of the most affectionate and outgoing young men you could ever wish to meet. From having no friends at all, he now has more than anyone else I know, with the exception of his grandfather, Malcolm.

Jim could be described as alternative. He has several piercings and a small dreadlock and he lives in a van called The Badger. After several career changes he is just about to start his final year at Norwich University where he is studying environmental science, and he came to stay with us before term began, to catch up with us and walk again on the farm which he loves so much, but also to find a garage which would give The Badger an MOT. He had tried in Norwich but decided that the quote he had had to put right all the things that were wrong with his mobile home was too expensive.

He and I spent an interesting two days, he driving The Badger from garage to garage in the hope that they would do the job and me following behind in the car to drive him home if someone – anyone – would accept it. It wasn't that it couldn't be done, it was usually that the parts wouldn't arrive until he was due back at university or that, once again, it was too costly. Finally we found the only garage – by this time in the wilds of Wiltshire – which was happy to do it in time and within budget but the entrance to its workshop was too low to drive The Badger in. We gave up and he went back to Norwich to get the job done at the garage which he had tried in the first place.

But it was lovely to be able to spend some time with him, albeit in somewhat bizarre circumstances.

Shortly afterwards we gave a temporary home to the other member of Maggie's beloved family, MooMoo the dachshund, while Maggie very admirably spent three weeks in Africa with a Christian mission. MooMoo's no trouble and regards Harcombe as her second home but I dreaded losing her should someone leave the garden gate open. She's pretty old and her legs are short, but she can move at a pace when she has a mind to do so. She would also be as much of a food thief as Gypsy, especially where cat food is concerned, but isn't as effective on account of being somewhat vertically challenged. I didn't lose her, and was very pleased to be able to play my part in helping Maggie fulfil a long held ambition.

September has surely been one of the sunniest on record. A truly lovely month.

A russet red the hazels gain,
As suited to their drear decline,
While maples brightest dress retain
And in their gayest colours shine.
The thorns and briars, vermilion hue,
Now full of hips and haws are seen.
If village prophesies are true,
They prove the winter will be keen.

John Clare ~ *Autumn*

A hedgerow in the valley

October

Autumn is here in all its glory. Harcombe Wood is golden and the creeper which grows riotously all over the front of the house glows with crimson leaves. There are berries everywhere – rose hips and hawthorn berries, purple sloes, my favourite pink and orange spindleberries and wild arums, which as children we called Lords and Ladies, have shed their tall green hoods and are laden with spikes of orange berries.

Contrary to earlier predictions when the rain just kept falling, this year's harvest has been an above average one. The sunny summer months have produced excellent crops which have been easy to gather in and now the fields are ploughed and drilled ready for next spring. Even the farmers are in relatively happy mood.

It's the time to say thank you to God for His bounty and we have done this at our Harvest Festival in Syde's tiny medieval church, singing our hearts out among the cabbages and chrysanthemums. This year, though, most of our contributions were in the form of non-perishable goods and will be given to the food bank in Cirencester where Christine is one of the main movers and shakers. In this wealthy, western democracy there are now people who cannot afford to buy food when they are between jobs or benefits and food banks have sprung up to support them. It's good to know what a particularly deserving cause our harvest gifts are going to.

Following on from the Harvest Festival, one of the most enjoyable events of the year is the Syde Harvest Supper which we have now hosted at Harcombe for over a decade. Everyone brings a contribution, either a casserole or a pudding, plus a bottle, we bake an oven full of potatoes and we all sit down together for an evening of friendship and enjoyment. It's just for the people who live in Syde or who have once lived there and loved it as we do, plus Val the vicar and retired clergyman Andrew, who takes many of our great services, helped by Sue and a selection of their animals. We used to sit at a long table in the covered yard – the Place of Parties – but as the autumn evenings closed in Malcolm would get very worried that people would be cold – which they usually were. Our decision to move into the house two years ago was an excellent one. What with the delicious food and wine and the wood burning stove, everyone is now slightly overheated but nobody seems to mind. It's a really fun evening and the easiest thing in the world to organise. I telephone the Wives of Syde as Malcolm calls them, tell them the date, ask "Same again?" with regard to the food

Autumn touches the trees around the farmhouse

and everyone turns up trumps. Part of the enjoyment is that we all like one another a lot. These are people we'd ask to a party whether they came from Syde or not.

I've never been an advocate of getting ready for Christmas too early but I always feel that the season of goodwill is inching closer when Malcolm announces that it's time to go and get the turkeys. By this he means that we're about to go, with several cardboard boxes in the back of the car, to a farm on the other side of Gloucester to buy turkey poults to rear at Harcombe for us and various members of the family to feast on during the festive season. Every year he agonises as to whether he'll do it again but every year we drive through woods blazing with autumn colour to Hyatt's farm in Brookthorpe and return with boxes of lively young turkeys in the back of our car. The Hyatts rear turkeys on a huge scale, as Malcolm himself used to do, but they have promised us just a few poults as long as we want them.

I always get enormous amusement from thinking how it must look to the average motorist driving behind this elderly couple in a quite smart, if rather muddy Ford Fiesta, to suddenly see white birds flapping about in the back. Because there's always at least one which wants to see beyond the confines of the cardboard box and escapes to view the passing scenery. The trouble is, it's not always possible to stop immediately and, by the time we've found a lay-by, the adventurous turkey has caused quite a stir. This year, after only one stop we got them all home and happily settled in what's always known as the Turkey House but which for the rest of the year serves as Splash's stable.

I have mixed feelings about rearing turkeys. There's nothing like a home-reared bird on Christmas Day but I do try not to think too deeply about where it has spent its final days and I never get too friendly with any of them.

For the first week of the month we had Maddi living with us, doing work experience at the stables. Her teacher did remark that it wouldn't be a new experience as she has been coming to Harcombe since she was eight but she certainly did plenty of work and was an enormous help to me. She spent the first day, however, going on his rounds with our vet, Mike, when she helped with the castration of two ponies and watched a complicated operation on a cat. She was also here to help me get all the ponies in for David and Alex, the farriers, and spent a morning watching them at work. As with Mike, they have been coming to us for years – I'd never dream of using anyone else – and they are good friends as well as excellent farriers. When one has finished and the other still has a pony to shoe I'll find the one who's waiting chopping wood for us. Maddi had to have her wits about her to keep up with the repartee, but she managed fine.

I did feel that I mustn't just use her as an extra pair of hands, so the following day, when Young Emily was here rather than at college, where she is in her second year of an equine course, I got her to give Maddi some basic lessons on first aid for horses. It was particularly fortunate that her teacher arrived to check on her progress just as she was putting a mock poultice on Pandora's foot and making a really good job of it. In fact, the teacher was rather impressed with the Harcombe set up and what Maddi had learned so far. So much so that, when she wrote to thank us for having her, she wondered if we might have someone next year...

Just after Maddi had gone home we had the first meeting of the Harcombe Society season. I always find it a defining moment in the Harcombe Year, rather as hunting and shooting people must feel about the start of the open season. I've never hunted a fox or shot a pheasant and I never want to, I'd so much rather see them running or flying around but for me, the first Harcombe meeting heralds the real start of autumn. The first speaker to kick off this season was a delightful man called Alan Macdonald who had spent his career working on V bombers during the Cold War. We usually find our speakers in a roundabout way and Alan came much recommended by his brother-in-law, retired vet Mick Ponting, one of our favourite neighbours and a very popular speaker last spring. It was a during a chance conversation that Mick mentioned him and we seized on the idea with enthusiasm, partly because it sounded so interesting (which it was) and partly because it put an end to what had become an ongoing argument between Malcolm and me.

When we had the annual general meeting of the Harcombe Society, Malcolm had said that he would like to get someone to speak about the English Civil War and some names whom we might contact were mentioned. Further investigation (by me), however, revealed that most of these speakers took either a Royalist or Republican view. This did not appeal to me as a former journalist – we always had it drummed into us that both sides must be represented equally – or as a lover of history. I have always felt that however much the Stuart monarchy needed to be constrained and that Cromwell was the man to do it, why, oh why did he name his simple son Richard to succeed him and start trying to create another dynasty? Malcolm will have none of this argument. For him Cromwell can do no wrong and he simply will not admit that his hero could ever make a mistake. I saw storm clouds ahead. Whoever we asked, one of us would be left cross or disappointed. Enter Alan to fill the gap and everyone was enthralled by his talk since almost all of us lived through the Cold War.

Towards the end of the month, Em brought the girls down for half term and to start cleaning the cottage next door and getting it ready for their arrival just before Christmas. Malcolm has very generously said that they can live there until they find somewhere else or stay there permanently if they really enjoy country living. Em had hired a large white van in order to bring down some of their furniture and the girls arrived full of excitement, having both ridden in the front seat and waved to other van drivers on the way. Young Emily's mum, Sharon, and brother Ben gave sterling help in taking the furniture up the awkward, winding stairs and Maddi's dad, Paul, arrived just in time to give a final shove to a very reluctant wardrobe.

The cottage was beginning to look really good. Janine and Littie both appeared to help at different times and between us we bundled most of the previous tenants' belongings into bin bags to return to them in due course. Em is a thorough and enthusiastic cleaner and the place has begun to sparkle as it never has before. I'm getting more and more excited about the prospect of having them here. In fact, I can hardly believe it's really going to happen.

During that week Daisy and Ruby were booked into Sapperton School for a taster day which worked very well because the half terms of Gloucestershire and Merseyside took place in different weeks. The two girls were not impressed, however, because they thought it wasn't any fun to have to go to school when they were supposed to be on holiday. As she drove them through the autumn lanes Em heard Ruby whisper to Daisy, "I'm scared." "So am I," replied her big sister. After school, though, it was a different story. They had made friends and really enjoyed themselves. And Em had met a friend from her sixth form days whose children are also at the school. Another hurdle successfully negotiated.

For some time I'd been noticing that Percy was looking his age – about 16, I think – he was moving more stiffly and his always immaculate thick white fur looked a little less gleaming. Percy was given to us by the local cattery when he was about a year old. He was so shy that they couldn't find him a domestic home and asked if we could have him to live the farm. They knew I was a responsible cat owner (and a soft touch) since we already had several of their cats at Harcombe.

In spite of my love of cats, I couldn't get close to him so I decided to leave him alone and see what happened and this went on for several years. Then Lorna arrived with her horse Jack and started a friendship with Percy who she sometimes managed to stroke and who by this time had begun to follow me around when I was out in the yard. He would also appear behind me when I was calling for one of the other cats as if to say, "I'm here. Will I do?" I realised that out of our five cats he was the most friendly towards all the others. He was not afraid of fierce

Top Cat Crocodile and Croc never went for him because he was never a rival. He was good mates with ginger-and-white Chance and he loved Blackadder, curling up to sleep beside him, the pair of them looking like adjacent piano keys. When Chance was killed on the road and Blackadder had to be put to sleep he took up with Eliot, an elderly, portly cat who we gave a home to when his owners went abroad. Eliot was the most gregarious of cats, mixing happily with his own kind and making it known that he was on for any party given by humans, provided there was plenty of food around. He attended one such event – a barbecue for my newsroom colleagues at the Wilts and Glos Standard – and then disappeared. We searched and searched with no success and I assumed – rightly as it turned out – that he had simply gone to sleep after the party and never woken up. What a great way to go. We found him, perfectly preserved, the next spring when we were moving stuff around prior to yet another party.

By this time Percy had got pretty fed up with his pals dying around him and decided to poke his nose round the kitchen door. He obviously liked what he saw because from that moment he became one of the inside cats ready to be fussed and petted like the rest of them, though he drew the line at sitting on anyone's knee. He had never been house trained but never once did he make a mess in the house and quickly learned to use the cat flap like the rest of them.

Apart from a spell of mysterious fits which did not last for long, he had never had a day's illness and had never visited the vet. In fact, he had never left the farm since the day he arrived. So when one weekend he went off his food, began to cough and sneeze and didn't venture outside, I rang Mike, the vet, and explained that I couldn't face traumatising him by putting him in a cat basket and taking him down to the surgery. Mike, bless him, came to the farm and after examining Percy, decided that he had picked up an infection, which was much worse due to his age, and that his system was beginning to fail. He offered to take him back to the surgery, put him on a drip and see if he improved but we both knew what my response was going to be. Animals have such an advantage over human beings in that they don't have to be kept alive when their quality of life has gone. "I'd much rather you put him to sleep," I said. "He's been a great cat and he's had a good life. Let's do it now." So we did. On the kitchen table where he had spent much of his later life sleeping.

Brian (is there no end to the things we rely on him to do?) came to dig a grave for him in the copse at the bottom of the garden near Croc, Oliver, Blackadder, Chance, Eliot and Barney, Chester and Phoebe, the whippets, Lily the Lurcher and Liz's Labradors, Misha, Mole and Lucy. I so miss seeing his white form around the farm and hearing his comforting mieow. Freya, our little grey tabby, was distraught when he didn't answer her call and mewed round the farm miserably for days. I soon realised that she has a bit of a hard time from her male companions. But not from Percy who never chased her, never lay in wait and jumped out at her. Who was her friend. Bless his heart.

Weatherwise, this month was how all Octobers should be.

Frosty mornings and still warm days, starry nights and autumn colours in abundance. Harcombe at its most glorious.

The dead leaves drift down on the headland,

The grey clouds sweep over the hill,

The dog and his master are ploughing

The stubble that's standing in drill.

Frank Mansell ~ *Autumn Ploughing*

fog clings to the fields

November

Funny old month, November, the link between the natural glory of October and the man-made razzle dazzle of December and Christmas. A month of falling leaves and the smell of bonfire smoke, of brown fields, ploughed and drilled, of dark evenings and, in our case, roaring log fires.

For several years we've had a wood burning stove in our kitchen/sitting room – but it never seemed to throw out much heat. It may have been protesting against the treatment meted out to it by Malcolm who insisted on filling it with logs and then forcing its doors shut, eventually breaking the seals and occasionally cracking the glass panes. I kept suggesting that maybe less wood would be a good idea but he couldn't bring himself to just let the fuel glow, it had to be roaring up the chimney. It also smoked badly from time to time, turning the kitchen walls to an unattractive shade of brownish grey.

When Malcolm makes a decision, he doesn't waste time. As

soon as he had decided that the wood burner had run its course, we had it removed and now our original fireplace is back in action, roaring away and keeping us warmer than we have been for years. It's lovely.

Why, we keep asking ourselves, did we abandon it in the first place?

The November meeting of the Harcombe Society was both unusual and highly successful. It was a demonstration of book binding and book production by our neighbours Lorna and Jeremy. They are an extraordinary couple for whom very little seems impossible. When Lorna had the novel she had written turned down by several publishers she decided to publish it herself. She spent a lot of time finding out just how it was done and armed with this information she and Jeremy created a traditionally bound book which could not be distinguished from one which had been mass produced, only it had much nicer bindings. We were very touched when they gave us copy number 8 as our last year's Christmas present and since then their business has really taken off – Lorna has written another novel and Crumps Barn Studio publishing is now really getting established. It certainly all goes on at Harcombe.

As summer gave way to autumn I was becoming increasingly anxious about Freddie, the little black pony we acquired several years ago for the ever growing girls to ride. He was a lovely chap who, though not without his own brand of quirkiness, was happy to do whatever was asked of him and refused point blank to quarrel with any of his equine companions, turning his back on them and walking off if anyone wanted to pick a fight. He was a gem.

Guessing that by now he was in his thirties, I knew he had several health issues which included a heart murmur and cataracts in each eye. They didn't stop him being ridden gently and this he still enjoyed. He loved his food and had a good appetite but I began to worry that he was losing weight even while there was still a bit of grass in the fields, probably because his teeth were also in a poor state. But I put these worries to the back of my mind.

During the second weekend in November, Amelia came for her first sleepover at Harcombe. I had promised her that she could come when Daisy and Ruby were here but I wanted to have her on her own first to see how she got on. She spent all Saturday with us and Young Emily and I took her out for a gentle ride on Freddie who behaved absolutely as normal. When we got back we put him and the others to bed and then Amelia had tea and went very happily to bed herself, exhausted by the day's activities with the horses and the 'big girls'.

Every night I go to check the ponies who are stabled before I go to bed, working on the principal drummed into me by an old friend, that if they're OK at midnight and sick in the morning, they haven't been sick for long. All the years I've done it, I've never been faced with a crisis – until now.

Even before I turned on the stable light I thought it odd that Freddie wasn't nickering over the stable doors, looking for the statutory peppermints. When I went in I found him collapsed on the floor. He got up, staggered about and then collapsed again, this time in front of the stable door so that I couldn't get out. When he next struggled to his feet I managed to move him away from the door and went to get Malcolm to stay with him while I phoned the vet.

Luckily Elise, who doesn't live very far away, was on call and it wasn't long before I saw her car lights glistening on the wet road. Even before she came, I was pretty sure of the outcome.

She tested his heart and found it in a very bad state, "What do you want me to do, Di?" she asked. I knew what my answer was going to be even though I didn't want to hear myself say it. It was Percy all over again. And so soon after. "I think we should put him down now before he suffers any more. He's had a good life and he's been such a star. It's the least we can do for him." It was absolutely the right, the only decision. His heart stopped almost as soon as he had the injection and he was instantly at peace. As with every other vet in that wonderful practice, Elise is as sympathetic to her patients' owners as to the patients themselves and several days later I received a lovely card with a horse's head just like Freddie's, signed by all the equine vets.

The next problem was how to tell Amelia who had, thank goodness, slept soundly through all the drama. What an awful thing to happen on her first ever sleepover... Next morning I rang Liz to ask how she felt I should handle it. "Just take her and show her Freddie. She's only recently seen Lucy (their Labrador) and before that Mole (their other Labrador) after they were put to sleep and she was fine as long as she was able to

Freddie looked after Maddi at her first show, and Chloe a year later

say goodbye." She was absolutely right. I told Amelia what had happened, reminding her what a lovely time the two of them had had yesterday, and, hand in hand, we walked across the yard to Freddie's stable where he lay as if asleep. "Bye bye, Freddie," said Amelia, stroking his soft black coat. Very matter of fact. And when Liz and Ian came to collect her, she ran out to them saying, "Mummy, Daddy, you must come and say goodbye to Freddie." Which they did. She has been absolutely fine about it and I'm sure it's because she was able to see him. Daisy and Ruby, however, were very sad, mainly, I think, because they weren't here. Thank goodness that state of affairs will soon be resolved.

Dear Freddie. I can hardly write this without shedding a tear. We all miss him a lot, he was so much a part of the Harcombe horsey scene. But when I'm feeling sad about him, and I do, I remember the wise words of my dear friend Anne Knowles, now long dead, who taught me most of what I know about horses and a lot more besides. "You just know, Di, when their time has come." And she was right. It was Freddie's time. His death was as graceful as his long life.

I honestly thought that we had our share of recent deaths among the livestock at Harcombe and up till now the turkeys had been growing apace and causing no anxiety. Then Malcolm found one dead, followed the next day by another. He was convinced that it was rats that had killed them and embarked on a determined – and expensive – campaign to eradicate them. Meanwhile, we moved the remaining turkeys to one of the stables so that he could spread the rat poison in the turkey house. He went to great lengths to make the stable rat-proof and we returned to Mr Hyatt, the turkey breeder, to buy another bird. More fun and games in the back of the car as the now much bigger turkey flapped about. The trouble was that when we put her in with the others they started to attack her so we moved her to another stable, gradually introducing her to her unfriendly companions one by one.

The stable yard became almost free of rats – certainly we found a lot of bodies – but ratus ratus doesn't give up that easily and the survivors soon made their way across the road to the hen run. The remaining hens, Nancy and Jessica, would be more than a match for a rat but the rats were eating all the hen food and moving nearer and nearer to the house. There was nothing for it but to move the hens to yet another stable while we dealt with the rats. That made three stables occupied by poultry – it was getting difficult to find places for all the horses...

But Malcolm's tactics seem to have worked and the yard and hen run are now almost rat free with only the bold survivors making the occasional appearance. I should say here, that we hate killing any animal and we both have a sneaking admiration for rats which are both intelligent and socially well adjusted (to other rats) but when it comes to losing our Christmas dinner, there's no argument.

At the end of the month Em and the girls came on their final trip before they actually move into the cottage and they and Janine stayed there overnight. We went in to join them for a glass of wine and the whole place looked so cheerful and cosy with the lights and candles which Em had arranged. I just can't wait for them to be here for good. The next morning we went and gathered holly and ivy from the farm and decorated the cottage so that it will be ready when they arrive the weekend before Christmas. All they need is a tree which I will get when I collect ours.

Time was when Malcolm would climb one of the huge fir trees on the farm, cut off the top and bear it into the house in triumph but he's got a bit old for that sort of adventure and now we buy ours from some delightful people who grow and sell trees to raise money for their wild animal sanctuary. Their trees are really nice and we like to feel that it's for a good cause but I know Malcolm misses the excitement.

Because autumn came late this year and the leaves didn't fall until November, Gypsy and I have had enormous fun scrunching through Harcombe Wood where the leaves make a thick carpet on the track. I don't think I'll ever get over my childish delight of running through leaves and I love to see views that I haven't seen all summer now that the trees are bare.

But my greatest childish delight, which has never waned, is my love of Christmas and I'm now looking forward to all the fun of it – and even the hard work too. At one time I never started preparations until December but now, with our ever increasing family, I try to do a few things in advance. I've made my present list – which always alarms me by its length – made sure that all the usual suspects will be here for Christmas lunch (they will, plus a few more because Em and the girls will be here for Christmas day this year), planned a few meals because our Christmas extends far beyond the actual day and actually bought several presents. Our cards have been printed with the picture of all the girls, horses, goats, cats, dog, Malcolm and me in the stable yard bright with the hanging baskets (a huge success), which Jeremy took in the summer, and are ready to go. Malcolm is getting in his usual tizzy about writing them (between us we send about two hundred cards) and I point out that he has put so much text inside that he only has to write his name. We have this discussion every year, but he feels obliged to keep up the tension.

The shops are filled with gifts of every sort, Christmas markets are appearing as if from nowhere, most towns have strung up their lights and there are about 25 more shopping days to go. Every year in our secular and materialistic society it becomes more and more difficult to keep one's sights set on the baby in the manger and all that Christmas should really mean.

But here at Harcombe, as well as having a really happy time, that's exactly what we shall do.

For unto you is born this day in the city of David
A saviour which is Christ the Lord.
And this shall be a sign unto you:
Ye shall find the babe wrapped in swaddling clothes,
Lying in a manger.

(Luke, ch. 2)

Charlie shares his stable with all who need it

December

I'm always convinced that December will be a month of glistening frosts, bright, thin sunshine and pale blue skies. It seldom is, but I just go on believing. This year it couldn't have been more different, wet and windy and unseasonably warm.

My Granny, who was a very wise woman with a fund of traditional sayings, used to declare that you should never eat Brussels sprouts until after the first frost. Malcolm, who is as addicted to sprouts as he is to broad beans and would eat them every day, given the chance, would have had to wait a long time this year if I had kept to her dictum and actually, they're fine without the frost. I expect they're grown in artificially cold conditions unheard of in Granny's day.

Always conscious that Christmas is getting ever closer, I've got quite a lot of my plans under way. Our cards were written early this month and it wasn't too difficult – in spite of constant complaints from Malcolm and threats to send no cards next year (he doesn't mean it, he couldn't manage without worldwide comments from his friends' that ours is the best card they ever have and they can never wait to receive it). I've bought most of the presents and put a large piece of ham and some smoked salmon in the deep freeze. The turkeys are now much too big for the few remaining rats to attack and, although they don't know it, the countdown to killing and plucking has begun. I absolutely hate the idea of it but I do love fresh, free range turkey.

But before we got too deep into the festive preparations, the last Harcombe Society meeting of this year took place. Professor Richard Holdaway came for the third year running to talk to us about the latest developments in space. He is a remarkable man who is professor of space technology, not only at two top British universities but also at the University of Bejing. I remembered this when we saw a newsflash, reporting that the Chinese were about to put robots on the moon. "I bet Richard knows all about this," I said to Malcolm and suddenly, there he was being interviewed on television – from China. This man, who seems to really enjoy the eccentricity of the Harcombe Society is one of the very top scientists in his field. He flew back from Bejing in the company of the prime minister, David Cameron, and various other big wigs and two days later he was on the phone to me, checking details for his visit to Syde at the end of the week.

As always, his lecture, with many fascinating illustrations, mostly of things which have occurred only the last week, was a cracking success. Space isn't my greatest interest, it all seems too vague and far away, but when he tells us about it, it's real and understandable and magical – and now. We had a great evening, finishing with wine and mincepies and set Richard on his way, hoping to see him again next year.

However much Christmas is on our minds, Amelia's birthday, on December 15, comes first and this year Liz and Ian organised a lunch party for about 40 people here at Harcombe. It was very good fun but very noisy and Malcolm retreated to the cottage next door when he had had his lunch, while the rest of us cleared away. Amelia loved it, especially as her little friend George, born just a few days after her, was here to enjoy it with her.

As soon as the birthday celebrations were over, I got cracking on the decorations which, though I'm far from being either artistic or innovative, I do regard as a bit of an art form. Most of the decorations come from somewhere on the farm. We really do deck the hall with boughs of holly (fah la la la la fah la la la) but also with a lot of purple berried ivy which is much easier to work with. I always try to set aside a day in which to do these decorations but it never works, because people keep calling and it's always, always, people that I want to see. This year Louise and Steve arrived just as I'd dragged a load of evergreen into the hall and I kept thinking, "Never mind, I'll do it tomorrow instead." The trouble is that the number of tomorrows is diminishing quickly. And it didn't help this year that it took me ages to untangle the Christmas tree lights. Much as I tried there was always a bit that was knotted up until in the end I just threw them about the tree and they looked fine. By the time that they fused just before Christmas, I really didn't care any more. I didn't have time to fix them and, in any case, the other set, which had given me no trouble, was twinkling away merrily. With Malcolm's help, I put up the tree we had bought for Em and the girls in the cottage but left it for them to decorate – and sort out their own lights...

But Malcolm's main concern was to get the turkeys killed and plucked and to give them time to hang for ten days. The secret, he says, is in the hanging. The turkey plucking always goes on in Charlie's stable and this puzzled me during my first Christmas at Harcombe. Why use a stable which is already in use every night when there are so many empty buildings on the farm? The answer was simple. Turkeys had been killed and plucked in that building, formerly a cow shed, ever since the Whitakers came to Harcombe and that was where they would continue to be plucked. Useless to argue, but I did request that the feathers should be cleared up afterwards. It was Malcolm's turn to be mystified. Wouldn't Charlie like a nice feather bed? Absolutely not.

Because Johnny hasn't been well and Malcolm is beginning to feel his age, Brian – there really is no end to his talents – and Malcolm's grandson Ollie took over the plucking this year with Malcolm offering advice which I'm not sure they needed... Then came ten days of more tension while in Malcolm's imagination wicked thieves or thieving rats would somehow get into the stable where the turkeys were hanging behind a door reinforced with two bolts and two padlocks. He wasn't satisfied until his daily inspection revealed that they were all still there.

My concern to get everything done was rather more concentrated this year as I had arranged with Em that I would help her move into the cottage, while she left the girls to celebrate an early Christmas with their dad, Dave, and his family before collecting them the day before Christmas Eve.

The move went relatively smoothly, the men arriving early so that they could unload the stuff for the cottage and then take the rest to a lock up garage in Cirencester, all during daylight hours. By 2.30pm they were on their way back north with most things in place except for Em's bed which they couldn't get up the winding staircase. Em arrived that evening and we spent the next day unpacking and sorting out what seemed like a mountain of their possessions. Brian – as ever – came to the rescue over the bed, taking it apart and reassembling it upstairs. By the time darkness fell, we were opening a bottle of wine in Em's new home and she went to sleep in her own bed in her own bedroom. I was actually beginning to believe that at last it was all happening.

She set off back to collect the girls after a jolly lunch at The Highwayman pub just up the road with the horsey girls and their parents. We did this last year too and it's becoming something of a tradition. We all exchanged presents and Malcolm and I left for the carol service at North Cerney chapel.

I was not filled with tidings of comfort and joy as I watched the weather forecast that evening. Gale force winds and driving rain were predicted for the next day. Surely nothing could stop Em and the girls getting here now?

But my fears were unfounded and after a night during which I hardly slept due to both worry and excitement, my little ones appeared out of the storm in time for lunch. They were here at Harcombe at last and for good!

There followed one of the best Christmasses ever – coincidentally my 20th at Harcombe – where our large family was all together for the first time. Christmas Eve turned out to be all I could have wished, culminating in the Christingle Service at Winstone Church where Em, Daisy, Ruby and I turned up, thinking we would probably know no one. We knew almost everyone! The girls were met at the door by some of the children they meet each year at Pony Camp and whisked off to the front of the church to take part in the Christingle. As we sang carols and listened to the Christmas story, I was so happy that I could feel tears welling up – and I don't often cry – I could hardly believe that I'd got my family here at last.

The stars were shining (for once) as we got back to Harcombe, still singing the carols, and very ready for the egg and chips which is our traditional Christmas Eve supper. Great excitement in anticipation of tomorrow, not least from me. We hugged each other good night and the girls went home to bed while I sorted out the turkey for tomorrow.

Christmas Day dawned bright and clear and, after I had put our turkey in the oven, we all trouped down to Syde Church for Christmas Morning service. I find Syde Church one of the holiest places in which I have worshipped. Maybe it's the ancient-ness of it and the fact that people from Syde have said prayers and sung hymns here for more than seven hundred years, but mostly, I think it's the fact that we all really enjoy worshipping together. It's very different from any other church I know – where else would the congregation peer at their order of service by gaslight, huddling together to keep warm in temperatures which make every exhalation of breath look like a puff of smoke? The doors of the box pews expand in winter, making entrance and exit difficult, the organ has its own eccentricities, responding only to an organist who knows it well, and the bell can't be rung because barn owls nest in the belfry. The story of the Angel Gabriel appearing to the shepherds and the baby born in the manger have real meaning here. "Oh, come all ye faithful... to Bethlehem."

This Christmas service was even more special than usual since Ruby had been asked to be the Virgin Mary – and ride on a real donkey – while Daisy was a shepherd in charge of two real sheep. Andrew took the service in which everyone played a part. Mine was to help Sue with the livestock. All went well in the church but when we took the animals outside Gentle the Donkey, who taken part in several Christmas services already, decided she had had enough, pulled away from Sue, nearly knocking her over and made off down the church path. Quick as a flash Daisy, who used to be so nervous of big animals, set off in hot pursuit, shepherd's costume streaming behind her, caught her and brought her back and we returned to the church for the end of the service with the rest of the congregation quite unaware of the drama outside. At the end we all sang the Gloucestershire

Gentle the donkey with her young escort at the Christmas service

Wassailing Song and then, because Phil was too frail to come to church this year, we all processed through the village to Gay and Phil's cottage and sang it again, much to their delight.

Back home, after breakfast, for which Em made delicious American pancakes, and after various proddings of the turkey, our guests began to arrive. Sally and Antony, Liz, Ian and Amelia, Janine, who always spends Christmas with us her adopted family, Maggie and her friend Carol who was on her own for Christmas, Em, Daisy and Ruby, Malcolm and I – thirteen of us in all. We drank sparkling wine when Malcolm welcomed everyone, especially the new neighbours, and then we set about the meal. The turkey was done to a turn, much to my relief – it's always guesswork – and we still had room for the puddings, contributed by Ian and Em.

When we had cleared away it was time to open the presents.

Daisy, Ruby and Amelia had been very patient but they just couldn't wait to open the pile of parcels stacked under the tree. Amelia is a dab hand at distribution and it wasn't long before the floor was covered with torn paper and tangled string.

At last we had diminished the huge pile until just the presents for tomorrow's guests remained. Darkness fell and those who weren't staying went on to another gathering while we prepared for a blissfully quiet evening at home. Cousin Martin arrived out of the night, having spent the day with Tom and his family. It's never quite Christmas until he appears, he is universally loved by for his great good nature and whimsical quirkiness. Time was when he would be accompanied by Hilary, whose death two years ago left a great hole in my very small family. We miss her for all sorts of reasons but particularly, at this time of year, for playing carols on our ancient piano, telling us how much better it would sound if we had it tuned...

I do love Christmas Day but I enjoy Boxing Day even more. The tension has disappeared, no one has to be anywhere by a certain time – and Boxing Day food is second to none – cold turkey, cold ham, baked potatoes, Janine's famous vegetable curry, lots of salad and delicious left over puddings. Best of all, this is our special Christmas celebration with Kate and Simon who come laden with lots of exotic food, most of it made by Kate – and a great deal of booze – and this year Jimbo, resplendent with tinsel threaded dreadlock, also arrived with Jess, his girlfriend. It's so good to see them all and to be able to spend time with them rather than wondering when the turkey is going to be ready. Then, after much eating and drinking there's more present opening – this year I've been given six exotic scarves, three lovely tops, several books and some much needed perfume and I'm thrilled to bits. Malc also has clothes, books and an awful lot of whisky...

Kate is delighted to have Em and the girls so much closer and we look forward to plenty of trips to the Big Smoke. She and Simon, who always adds his special niceness to our family celebrations and is a great favourite with Daisy and Ruby, stayed a day longer than usual and were entertained by the new neighbours as well as by us. I hated saying goodbye to them after such a lovely time but this time it wasn't as if the house was suddenly empty and everyone had disappeared.

So the year drew to its inevitable close. As years go, it's been a good one, especially in its final outcome and I still can hardly believe that I have three of my family living next door after years of visits and sad goodbyes.

Traditionally, after all the family razmataz, we spend a relatively quiet New Year with Chris, Johnny and Anne and one of their many cousins, also John, at one of our homes. This year it was our turn to be hosts at Harcombe but, since Johnny had been poorly just before Christmas, I cooked the food at home and we took it all to their house to eat. It was another evening of family conviviality, since we all have a great affection for one another, and as midnight struck, we joined hands in our tiny circle to sing Auld Lang Syne.

What will next year bring, I wonder?

Gloucestershire Wassail

(Note: Cherry and Dobbin are horses.
Broad May and Fillipail are cows)

Wassail, wassail all over the town!
Our toast it is white, and our ale it is brown,
Our bowl is made of the white maple tree;
With the wassailing bowl we'll drink to thee.

So here is to Cherry and his right cheek,
Pray God send our master a good piece of beef,
And a good piece of beef that may we all see;
With the wassailing bowl we'll drink to thee.

And here is to Dobbin and to his right eye,
Pray God send our master a good Christmas pie,
And a good Christmas pie that may we all see;
With our wassailing bowl we'll drink to thee.

So here is to Broad May and to her broad horn,
May God send our master a good crop of corn,
And a good crop of corn that may we all see;
With the wassailing bowl we'll drink to thee.

 I

And here is to Fillipail and to her left ear,
Pray Good send our master a happy New Year,
And a happy New Year as e'er he did see;
With the wassailing bowl we'll drink to thee.

Then here's to the maid in the lily white smock,
Who tripped to the door and slipped back the lock!
Who slipped to the door and pulled back the pin,
For to let these jolly wassailers in.

* * * * * * * * *

Wassailing is thought to have its origins in Anglo Saxon England around the time of Beowulf. Wes hal , meaning Good Health, was a form of greeting used on a festive occasion. Wassailing, which originally was a blessing for the next year's crops, usually took place around Christmas and the winter solstice and was a good way of lighting up a cold winter's night with a bit of revelry as well.

Around the sixteenth and seventeenth centuries working people would go round the big houses with a wassailing bowl made from hardwood, which would be filled with beer or cider for a winter celebration and a blessing of the crops.

This tradition continued until the Great War when many of the big houses ceased to exist in their original form and today's celebrations, which take place mainly in the apple growing areas of the west country, are mainly revivals and the blessing is for the cider apple crops.

Our friend Eric Freeman, a farmer and a very active member of the Gloucestershire Farmers' Friends, holds a Wassail at his home near Newent every year around Twelfth Night. It's a scene straight from a Thomas Hardy novel, but with its origins in pagan times and with a Christian touch as well. Eric, in farmer's smock and breeches is in charge of proceedings, a wire basket filled with straw is set alight to replicate the sun and make sure that it will come back after the winter gloom, a gun is fired over the apple orchard to drive evil spirits from the trees and a prayer is said, just to make sure. The wassail bowl is filled, a lot of cider is drunk and a good time is had by all. "It's a good excuse for a party," says Eric. And, of course, that's what it has always been.

The End